Children's Conceptions of Spatial Relationships

Robert Cohen, *Editor*

NEW DIRECTIONS FOR CHILD DEVELOPMENT
WILLIAM DAMON, *Editor-in-Chief*

Number 15, March 1982

Paperback sourcebooks in
The Jossey-Bass Social and Behavioral Sciences Series

Jossey-Bass Inc., Publishers
San Francisco • Washington • London

Children's Conceptions of Spatial Relationships
Number 15, March 1982
    Robert Cohen, *Editor*

New Directions for Child Development Series
William Damon, *Editor-in-Chief*

New Directions for Child Development (publication number
USPS 494-090) is published quarterly by Jossey-Bass Inc., Publishers.
Second-class postage rates are paid at San Francisco, California,
and at additional mailing offices.

Correspondence:
Subscriptions, single-issue orders, change of address notices,
undelivered copies, and other correspondence should be sent to
New Directions Subscriptions, Jossey-Bass Inc., Publishers,
433 California Street, San Francisco, California 94104.

Editorial correspondence should be sent to the Editor-in-Chief,
William Damon, Department of Psychology, Clark University,
Worcester, Massachusetts 01610.

Library of Congress Catalogue Card Number LC 81-48564
International Standard Serial Number ISSN 0195-2269
International Standard Book Number ISBN 87589-875-0

Cover art by Willi Baum
Manufactured in the United States of America

Ordering Information

The paperback sourcebooks listed below are published quarterly and can be ordered either by subscription or single-copy.

Subscriptions cost $35.00 per year for institutions, agencies, and libraries. Individuals can subscribe at the special rate of $21.00 per year *if payment is by personal check.* (Note that the full rate of $35.00 applies if payment is by institutional check, even if the subscription is designated for an individual.) Standing orders are accepted.

Single copies are available at $7.95 when payment accompanies order, and *all single-copy orders under $25.00 must include payment.* (California, Washington, D.C., New Jersey, and New York residents please include appropriate sales tax.) For billed orders, cost per copy is $7.95 plus postage and handling. (Prices subject to change without notice.)

To ensure correct and prompt delivery, all orders must give either the *name of an individual* or an *official purchase order number.* Please submit your order as follows:

Subscriptions: specify series and subscription year.
Single Copies: specify sourcebook code and issue number (such as, CD8).

Mail orders for United States and Possessions, Latin America, Canada, Japan, Australia, and New Zealand to:
Jossey-Bass Inc., Publishers
433 California Street
San Francisco, California 94104

Mail orders for all other parts of the world to:
Jossey-Bass Limited
28 Banner Street
London EC1Y 8QE

New Directions for Child Development Series
William Damon, *Editor-in-Chief*

CD1   *Social Cognition,* William Damon
CD2   *Moral Development,* William Damon
CD3   *Early Symbolization,* Howard Gardner, Dennie Wolf
CD4   *Social Interaction and Communication During Infancy,* Ina C. Uzgiris
CD5   *Intellectual Development Beyond Childhood,* Deanna Kuhn
CD6   *Fact, Fiction, and Fantasy in Childhood,* Ellen Winner, Howard Gardner
CD7   *Clinical-Developmental Psychology,* Robert L. Selman, Regina Yando
CD8   *Anthropological Perspectives on Child Development,* Charles M. Super, Sara Harkness
CD9   *Children's Play,* Kenneth H. Rubin
CD10 *Children's Memory,* Marion Perlmutter
CD11 *Developmental Perspectives on Child Maltreatment,* Ross Rizley, Dante Cicchetti
CD12 *Cognitive Development,* Kurt W. Fisher

CD13 *Viewing Children Through Television,* Hope Kelly, Howard Gardner
CD14 *Childrens' Conceptions of Health, Illness, and Bodily Functions,* Roger Bibace, Mary E. Walsh

Contents

Editor's Notes: The Understanding of Large-Scale
Spatial Cognition
Robert Cohen

1

Chapter 1. Spatial Cognition as a Function of Size and Scale
of the Environment
David L. Weatherford

5

Much of the contemporary interest in large-scale spatial cognition evolved from research using small tabletop models. This move to more ecologically relevant environments raises the issue of compatibility of findings across environments that differ in size and/or scale.

Chapter 2. The Familiarity Factor in Spatial Research
Linda P. Acredolo

19

Familiarity with an environmental setting can be understood as an independent variable (a cause of increased knowledge) or as a dependent variable (a result of increased knowledge). The concept of familiarity is examined in both senses, with suggestions for elaborating the cognitive/social/emotional dimensions that underlie the concept.

Chapter 3. The Organization of Route Knowledge
Gary L. Allen

31

The study of the development of spatial cognition has important implications for other work in cognitive development (and vice versa). The author's research on the organization of route knowledge is used to exemplify the potential cross-fertilization of research interests.

Chapter 4. The Role of Activity in the Construction of
Spatial Representations
Robert Cohen

41

Since multiple views are necessary in order to fully apprehend the space in large-scale environments, the role of physical activity in the environment is presumed to be a critical factor for large-scale spatial cognition. A program of research investigating the influence of walking for the buildup of spatial representations is presented and an elaboration of our views on the role of activity is suggested.

Chapter 5. Children's Large-Scale Spatial Cognition: Is the
Measure the Message?
Lynn S. Liben

51

Different spatial tasks provoke different results and hence different interpretations concerning underlying spatial representations. The relationship between spatial behaviors and spatial representations is examined. The author presents an important distinction between spatial thought and spatial storage and urges that cognitive strategies used to organize and extract spatial information be considered.

Chapter 6. Development of Spatial Cognition and Cognitive Development   65

Nora Newcombe

The study of the development of spatial cognition has evolved as a relatively independent area in the field of cognitive development. Compartmentalization has insulated researchers in the field from addressing other fundamental concerns of cognitive developmentalists. The author reviews the previous chapters and considers spatial cognition in terms of the general issues of stages of cognitive development, reasons for age-related cognitive changes, and the concept of microgenesis.

Chapter 7. Towards a Social Ecology of Cognitive Mapping   83

Alexander W. Siegel

In this chapter, an alternative perspective is offered for considering spatial cognition in particular and cognitive development in general. With this "new functionalism" view the author stresses the need for an examination of the contexts and situations encountered by children. The importance of social interactions and purposive functioning in the child's life are major focal points. In addition, the issue of criteria for performance based on adult or external standards is critically examined.

Index   95

Editor's Notes:
The Understanding of
Large-Scale Spatial Cognition

There is a kind of basicness to the study of spatial cognition and its ontogenesis. Philosophers have long speculated on the roots and nature of this knowledge (see Hart and Moore, 1973, and Siegel and White, 1975, for reviews of these theories). The focus of early developmental research was on the comprehension of spatial relations — the processes of spatial cognition. To this end, small tabletop models of environments were used to investigate, for example, the understanding of topological, projective, and Euclidean descriptions of spatial information. A rather substantial literature exists on the development of spatial abilities from these model studies.

Although reports examining spatial cognition of naturalistic settings could be found earlier, interest in the development of large-scale spatial cognition has been a relatively recent phenomenon, spawned to a great extent by the publication of Siegel and White's (1975) study. A variety of issues have been generated with this move to large-scale environments — issues that were either unimportant or inaccessible to researchers using model spaces. For example, since large-scale spaces surround the individual and require that he or she have multiple views to apprehend entirely their structure (Acredolo, 1981; Ittelson, 1973), how does the individual maintain an orientation despite circuitous paths and shifts in position? How are routes mentally constructed and manipulated where the terminus is not visible from the start? What activities, both physical and cognitive, promote the incorporation of spatial knowledge? What are the important parameters in the structure of, and activities in, an environment that facilitate one's wayfinding, familiarity, and social-emotional transactions?

The present volume, a product of a symposium presented at the meeting of the Society for Research in Child Development in Boston in April 1981, contains reports of several research programs examining some of the issues just mentioned. The first chapter, by David Weatherford, provides an introduction to the volume, examining the issues of size and scale of environments. This chapter provides a link from much of the previous model environment research to the research presented in the remaining chapters.

In the second chapter, Linda Acredolo examines the concept of familiarity. She notes that in its colloquial usage *familiarity* has been understood to mean either a result of increased environmental knowledge or a cause of that knowledge. While examining both senses of the concept, Acredolo also reports data implying that familiarity may serve its most significant function by providing emotional security.

In the third chapter, Gary Allen presents his research on the recognition of landmarks and the organization of landmarks into subdivisions of routes. The implications from research in other areas of cognitive development are applied to his findings.

My research on the role of activity is presented next. Large-scale environments necessitate multiple views of the space as noted; thus, from several theoretical perspectives, walking is believed to be a critical activity for the construction of spatial representations. The data from a number of studies are presented with the not surprising conclusion that walking is important for some children, some of the time. An expanded view of the role of activity is offered, one that stresses the functional value of the activity.

In the fifth chapter, Lynn Liben examines an issue that is critical to all the research presented here — the relationship between the spatial behaviors we assess and the spatial representations we infer from those behaviors. She addresses this competence-performance question and offers important conceptual distinctions. In addition, Liben urges researchers to consider the strategies used by children to organize and extract spatial information.

In the sixth chapter, Nora Newcombe reviews the previous chapters and spatial cognition research in the context of general cognitive development. She notes that until now researchers of spatial cognition have worked in relative isolation from the more general concerns of other cognitive developmentalists. The pros and cons of this continued isolation are discussed.

Finally, in the seventh chapter, Alex Siegel reviews the earlier chapters and suggests a new direction for future investigations. This new direction may be termed a "new functionalism." Siegel stresses the purposive nature of human behavior and the environmental contexts for those behaviors. The environment is more than just a physical arena for behavior — it provides the context and meaning for all behavior.

Several themes run through this volume. First, spatial cognition involves the complex interaction of (1) the nature of the environment, (2) physical/social/cognitive transactions in the environment, (3) tasks used to externalize knowledge of the space, and (4) the developmental status of the knower. Second, directions for the field of spatial cognition are addressed at two levels. Refinements for investigating and understanding spatial cognition are offered; at a more general level, propositions for the cross-fertilization of the field with other domains are presented. Finally, several authors propose that spatial cognition should not be viewed as solely a cognitive activity. In conjunction with examining the comprehension of spatial relations in the physical world, the social and emotional aspects of these contexts must also be considered.

Robert Cohen
Editor

References

Acredolo, L. P. "Small- and Large-Scale Spatial Concepts in Infancy and Childhood." In L. S. Liben, A. H. Patterson, and N. Newcombe (Eds.), *Spatial Representations and Behavior Across the Life Span.* New York: Academic Press, 1981.

Hart, R. A., and Moore, G. T. "The Development of Spatial Cognition: A Review." In R. M. Downs and D. Stea (Eds.), *Image and Environment: Cognitive Mapping and Spatial Behavior.* Chicago: Aldine, 1973.

Ittelson, W. H. "Environment Perception and Contemporary Perceptual Theory." In W. H. Ittelson (Ed.), *Environment and Cognition.* New York: Seminar Press, 1973.

Siegel, A. W., and White, S. H. "The Development of Spatial Representations of Large-Scale Environments." In H. W. Reese (Ed.), *Advances in Child Development and Behavior.* Vol. 10. New York: Academic Press, 1975.

Robert Cohen is an assistant professor of psychology at Memphis State University. In addition to working in the research program on the development of spatial cognition, he is also involved in research examining clinical and educational interventions in the context of developmental change.

Size and scale are not synonymous terms in the study of spatial cognition.
This chapter discusses these concepts, offering bases of integration
among diverse research findings in the area.

Spatial Cognition as a Function of Size and Scale of the Environment

David L. Weatherford

A variety of experimental and naturalistic environments have been used to examine how individuals process and store spatial information. Many researchers have used small tabletop spaces or models, while others have asked subjects to demonstrate their knowledge of spatial areas as large as cities. Researchers have also asked whether an individual's cognitive interactions with this assorted variety of environments are similar or whether such different types of spaces invoke different mental processes. This chapter addresses this issue.

The environmental features of size and scale will be analyzed here. The interest in size centers around what has been called the microspatial versus macrospatial distinction. The former term refers to small, tabletop models of space and the latter term signifies large, full-size environments. The term *scale* has been used in a variety of ways. While a few researchers have provided a definition of the concept, most have employed it as it is used in common conversational exchange, so that it is essentially synonymous with size. It is in this sense that researchers of various disciplines automatically refer to tabletop models as small-scale spaces and neighborhoods or cities as large-scale spaces. Yet an urban planner or geographer may think of a classroom as being small-scale, while developmental psychologists might consider it

R. Cohen (Ed.). *New Directions for Child Development: Children's Conceptions of Spatial Relationships*, no. 15.
San Francisco: Jossey-Bass, March 1982.

large-scale. Where a definition of scale has been offered, the criteria for a large-scale space has been twofold: (1) a person can move around within the space and (2) multiple vantage points must be occupied in order for the space to be apprehended in its entirety (Acredolo, 1981; Hazen, Lockman, and Pick, 1978; Siegel, 1981; Weatherford and Cohen, 1981). Use of this definition has led to at least two problems, however. First, researchers who label environments or spaces according to this definition often disagree on how these criteria should be applied. For example, Acredolo (1977), Herman (1980), and Herman and Siegel (1978) have used barrier-free spaces the size of an average classroom (or smaller) that they termed large-scale. Weatherford and Cohen (1981), on the other hand, refer to the same environments as small-scale spaces. Second, the two-part definition of scale given earlier can lead to some confusing and counterintuitive labeling of environments. For example, Siegel (1981) notes that the city of Pittsburgh can be termed small-scale according to this defintion if one can view the entire area from a single vantage point atop the U.S. Steel Building. In order to avoid this problem and make the definition conceptually more palatable, I would like to add a stipulation to the definition. That is, let us assume that the viewer in question is standing on the same plane as the spatial layout itself.

In this chapter, then, I will label as large-scale only that environment for which an observer standing on the same plane must occupy multiple viewing locations in order to visually extract all of the spatial information needed to generate an overall spatial representation. Given this defintion, there are three basic types of environments or spaces typically used in the study of spatial cognition: (1) model/small-scale, or tabletop model spaces that can be observed or manipulated only from the outside, (2) navigable/small-scale, or spaces that are large enough in size to permit travel but can still be viewed in entirety from a single vantage point, and (3) large-scale, or spaces that meet the criteria given earlier.

In this chapter, research on perspective taking and cognitive mapping is examined. The former is generally assessed in a situation where a subject is asked to mentally manipulate or transform spatial information that is available to the subject's view. Cognitive mapping more typically requires the subject to use spatial information not visually available but represented in the subject's memory. Studies on these two phenomena will be reviewed briefly for each of the three types of environments described. While some studies appear to assess both of these spatial abilities, each will be assigned to one category or the other based on the primary interest expressed by the investigator of the experiment and the explicit instructions given to the participants in the experiment.

Model/Small-Scale Spaces

Model spaces have been used in spatial cognition research in two ways. First, they have been used to serve as small environments to be mentally represented or manipulated according to particular task demands. The cognitive processing of the spatial information contained in the model is assumed to be isomorphic to what occurs in similar interactions with spatial aspects of the real-world environment. Second, model spaces often have been used as a means of allowing the subject to externalize spatial knowledge. The focus here is on research using model spaces (or environments) in the first way described — that is, models are analogues to study environmental cognition.

Perspective Taking. In the traditional perspective-taking situation (initiated by Piaget and Inhelder, 1967), a subject is asked to infer the view that another observer has of an object or array of objects. Assuming that the subject and the other observer occupy different viewing positions, the subject must determine how the object or objects and their spatial interrelationships appear to the second observer.

Piaget and Inhelder's model environment consisted of a miniature replica of three mountains, varying in height and further differentiated by color and landmarks (for example, animals, house). Other investigators have used mock replicas of naturalistic scenes (see, for example, Borke, 1975; Brodzinsky, Jackson, and Overton, 1972; Miller, 1967; Minnigerode and Carey, 1974; Shantz and Watson, 1971); arrays of unrelated, easily differentiable objects (Fishbein, Lewis, and Keiffer, 1972; Knudson and Kagan, 1977; Salatas and Flavell, 1976; Shlechter and Salkind, 1979); and model displays consisting of less differentiable objects (Eliot and Dayton, 1976; Fehr, 1980; Hoy, 1974; Liben, 1978; Nigl and Fishbein, 1974).

Perspective-taking ability develops from the very simple level of understanding *what* the other person sees to the more complex ability of inferring all dimensions of projective relations and how they are systematically transformed with the observer's positional change. The performance of children of various ages is dependent upon a complex interaction of stimulus display features, response demands, and procedural variables. Factors such as stimulus complexity, arrangement of objects, position of other observers, and mode of response have been shown to affect performance in a variety of perspective-taking studies (see Fehr, 1978; Shantz, 1975).

Cognitive Mapping. There have been very few studies where subjects were exposed to a small-scale model space and then required to demonstrate memory of the spatial interrelationships among the objects in the array. Two studies exemplifying this kind of research will be briefly described.

Watkins and Schadler (1980) examined the ability of kindergarten, first-grade, and third-grade children to employ a mnemonic strategy based on an object frame of reference. Children observed a model display of a zoo containing nine toy animals. Next, they were directed to replicate the zoo from memory on another model board. One group was instructed to use an organizational strategy based on the use of an object frame of reference. A second group of children was told of the organizational strategy but not prompted to use it. A third group was not told of the strategy. Results showed that the directed instructions had the greatest facilitative effect on the performance of the kindergarteners. Watkins and Schadler maintained that the instructions enabled the young children to attend to and organize the spatial information by using one or more of the animals in the array as a reference for locating the next. In addition, they hypothesized that the older children may have spontaneously employed an object frame of reference to organize spatial information, since placement accuracy scores for these children were as high in the control condition (no instructions) as in the strategy-instruction conditions.

Anooshian and Wilson (1977) investigated the influence of route extensity. Kindergarten and adult subjects were trained to remember the locations of four objects. During this training, some objects were connected by indirect, circuitous train tracks, others by direct tracks. Control subjects saw a display of objects connected only by direct train tracks (experimental group). Subjects were told to place the four objects on a response board (no tracks included) to reflect how they had been arranged on the original board. Analyses of the actual interobject distances revealed that children, though not adults, tended to overestimate distances between objects connected by indirect routes of travel.

Navigable/Small-Scale Spaces

The environments classified here as navigable/small-scale spaces have been referred to by investigators as large-scale spaces. It seems likely that this is the case because, for most investigators, large-scale has traditionally implied a big space relative to the small model spaces so prevalent in spatial cognition research.

Perspective Taking. Very few studies of perspective taking have used anything other than a model space. However, a few recent experiments have extended the study of perspective taking into a new and perhaps more ecologically valid kind of spatial setting. Weatherford and Cohen (1980) used a spatial area of 1.5m × 2.5m containing seven landmark objects. Although this was a rather small space, it did move the traditional perspective-taking task into a space in which one could move around and interact in various ways. The locomotor activity of third-graders was systematically varied prior to a standard picture-choosing perspectives task. Each child walked along one of two routes of observations — either inside or outside the delineated environment. In addition, one of two types of movement/interaction was included. Each child either moved nonstop about the environment, labeling each object sequentially, or stopped periodically along the route and labeled all objects in a systematic fashion. For males, perspective taking was facilitated in the *stop-look* movement/interaction groups. Also, for both sexes, the *stop-look* experience coupled with an outside route of observation led to fewer egocentric responses, such as choosing a picture depicting one's own view instead of the other observer's view.

Herman and Coyne (1980) examined perspective taking using an experimental environment that was 7.5m × 5m in size. Subjects were twenty, sixty, and seventy years old. A unique procedure designed by Hardwick, McIntyre, and Pick (1976) was used. The subject directed a pointer on a tripod at designated objects in the room. Perspective ability was required by having the subject stand at a location and imagine that he or she was standing at another location in the room. Then the subject was asked to point at various objects in the room as if he or she were actually at the imagined location. Herman and Coyne found that young adults were more accurate in this kind of perspective judgment than the elderly adults. In addition, subjects who were taken to each of the four target locations in the room prior to testing were more accurate in the task than subjects who did not have this experience.

Cognitive Mapping. Few studies have used navigable/small-scale spaces to investigate the ability of individuals to construct a spatial representation. Most of these have been studies that set up a special environment in a large room (for example, a classroom). At least one common interest among several of these investigations has been the role of locomotor movement. Herman and Siegel (1978) had kindergarteners, second-graders, and fifth-graders encounter a mock town set up in a 4.9m × 6.1m space easily viewed in its entirety from any location on the perimeter. In one experiment, the town was set up in a classroom and in a second experiment the mock town was in the center of a large gymnasium. The mapping task was to reconstruct the small town after the objects were removed. Comparing performance across the two settings, it was found that young children in the bounded space (classroom) were far more accurate in their performance than in the unbounded space (gymnasium), while older children's accuracy was relatively unaffected by this variable. Another variable looked at was travel. In one experiment, half the children at each grade level walked through the town three times and the other half stood at the starting point on the perimeter and only watched the experimenter walk through the town. Walking through the environment did not facilitate reconstruction relative to the looking-only experience.

Cohen, Weatherford, and Byrd (1980) performed a similar study in an average size classroom. The child either walked through the space or only viewed it from a stationary position on the periphery. However, there were two very important differences from the Herman and Siegel (1978) study. First, the walking experience here allowed considerably more travel among the landmarks in the environment. Second, the response measure was a distance estimation task for which subjects estimated all pairwise interpoint distances among locations. The findings in this study also showed that a no-movement experience could lead to performance equivalent to that following a travel experience. However, this was only true when the distance estimation task was congruent to the acquisition experience — that is, involved no locomotor movement on the part of the subject.

Herman (1980) tested kindergarteners and third-graders using the same mock town and reconstruction task employed by Herman and Siegel

(1978). In contrast to children in the earlier study, children who walked within the environment did better than those who only walked around the perimeter. Even better performance was demonstrated by children whose attention was directed to spatial relationships among the small buildings as they walked within the environment. In all three of these conditions, third-graders were more accurate than kindergarteners. In addition, reconstruction accuracy improved with repeated walks.

Large-Scale Spaces

Perspective Taking. Only one study to date has examined perspective-taking ability in a large-scale space. Hardwick, McIntyre, and Pick (1976) tested second-graders, fifth-graders, and adults in a familiar library. It seems unlikely that one could observe all the spatial relations contained in the room from one vantage point given all the potential occlusions (such as desks, bookshelves, card catalogue, and so forth). The perspective-taking task for Herman and Coyne (1980) has already been described. Because of a large opaque screen, half the children could not see the spatial array of landmarks as they tried to imagine various perspectives, while the other half could freely observe the room. The completeness and accuracy with which cognitive maps could be manipulated in this situation improved considerably with age. First-graders often utilized the simple strategy of egocentric localization, pointing to the target objects appropriate for their present location rather than for the imagined viewing position. This was especially true when their view of the spatial layout was not obstructed and they could freely view the objects from their current perspective. Fifth-graders were more likely to apply transformational rules to the spatial interrelationships in the room. They encountered difficulty in attempting to compute very specific spatial features such as angles and distances. College students were very accurate in their perspective judgments.

Cognitive Mapping. The early studies of the ability to cognitively represent large-scale spaces assessed individuals' spatial representations of naturalistic settings (see Piaget, Inhelder, and Szeminska, 1960; Shemyakin, 1962). This approach was followed up in the late 1960s and the 1970s by urban planners and geographers (for example, Appleyard, 1970; Ladd, 1970). It was typical to have children and adults draw maps or build small model representations to demonstrate their knowledge of locales of various sizes, from their neighborhood to their entire city.

Kosslyn, Pick, and Fariello (1974) introduced a different approach by constructing a large-scale experimental space. The space was a seventeen-foot square area sectioned into four quadrants by the combination of two opaque barriers (which precluded viewing of the entire space from a single viewpoint) and two transparent barriers. Ten landmarks were scattered throughout the space. Subjects were trained to walk from a home position on the perimeter to each of the ten landmarks in the space. Following this, they were asked to rank order the distances among the landmarks. Preschoolers overestimated the distance between locations separated by either type of barrier relative to estimates of distances between objects with no intervening barrier. Adults overestimated distances only between locations separated by opaque barriers. Kosslyn, Pick, and Fariello suggested that young children primarily rely upon functional distance considerations during their estimates of the physical distances; that is, they focus on the distance required to move from one location to the other. Adults, although influenced by functional distance, are able to rely on visual distance information available across the transparent barriers in determining physical distance. Cohen and Weatherford (1980, 1981) have also conducted studies using experimental environments to examine how locomotor movement, as well as barriers, influence children's representations of large-scale space. Cohen, Baldwin, and Sherman (1978) studied these variables in a large-scale naturalistic setting. This research is presented in detail in the chapter by Cohen in this volume.

Other studies have used large-scale spaces to examine how one's representation of a spatial layout is influenced by such things as one's pattern of travel (Hazen, Lockman, and Pick, 1978) and one's type of locomotion through space (Feldman and Acredolo, 1979). Several investigators have studied the issue of familiarity in very different settings, including a hallway (Acredolo, Pick, and Olsen, 1975), a classroom (Siegel and Schadler, 1977), and a school library (Cohen and others, 1979). See Acredolo's chapter in this volume for a more extensive discussion of the role of familiarity in spatial cognition.

Comparison Studies

Few studies have made direct comparisons of spatial behaviors observed in the three kinds of spaces identified in this chapter. Acredolo (1977) compared the ability to coordinate perspectives of a tabletop model and of a navigable/small-scale space. Although Acredolo labels the latter as large-scale, it does not meet the criteria for large-scale described here. The large space was a twelve- by twelve-foot room with no barriers to inhibit viewing in the room. Three-, four-, and five-year-olds were trained to find a small trinket hidden on either the left or right side of the room. Next, they were directed to move to the other end of the room so that they now had the reverse perspective. When asked to find the trinket now, they had to coordinate the two opposing views in order to determine its correct location. An analogous situation was designed using a two- by two-foot model board with three- and four-year-olds. Again, a trinket was hidden on either side and the child learned its location. The child then moved from a chair on one end of the table to a chair on the opposite side of the board. From this new perspective, the child was to locate the hidden trinket. A variable manipulated in both spaces was that of landmark differentiation. There were three conditions: no landmarks, landmarks at the two viewing locations, and landmarks at the two possible locations for the hidden trinket. The three- and four-year-old children performed much better in the perspective-coordination task when using the model space than in the large space when no landmarks were available. For the large space, these children found it more difficult to coordinate the two views under the no landmark condition relative to either of the landmark-present conditions. However, with the small model space, the no landmark condition was no more difficult than the landmark conditions. Acredolo (1977) proposed two possible explanations for the difference in performance with the two spaces. First, with the model space there was the possible advantage of viewing the spatial layout in the context of a larger environment (that is, the room). Second, the small size of the model space may have reduced memory demands by allowing the child to survey the entire set of spatial relations in a single glance. The findings of this study support the importance of the distinction made in this chapter between model/small-scale spaces and navigable/small-scale spaces.

Siegel and others (1979) compared children's cognitive maps of a large space and a small-scale model space. The large space was a navigable/small-scale mock town with an area of 4.6m × 6.1m. A similar layout was set up on a 81.3cm × 101.6cm model board with small color photos used to denote buildings. Spatial knowledge was tested by having children reconstruct the two in either the model space or the navigable/small-scale space. Thus, there were four conditions: (1) expose large–construct large (2) expose small–construct small (3) expose large–construct small and (4) expose small–construct large. Children were most accurate when tested in a space whose dimensions were similar to those of the space in which they acquired their spatial knowledge. Accuracy was significantly reduced only in the expose small–construct large condition. The authors maintained that "one may with caution generalize research findings from small-size models to actual real world spaces" (p. 584).

Weatherford and Cohen (1981) compared the performance of third- and fifth-graders on a spatial representation task after they encountered either a navigable/small-scale environment or a large-scale environment. The same 8.1m × 6.2m space containing six common objects as landmarks was used for both environments. The large-scale space was created by including three large opaque barriers that were placed to preclude viewing of the entire spatial array from a single vantage point. In conjunction with type of environment, Weatherford and Cohen manipulated the type of acquisition experience by having children either view the space by walking through the spatial area or by only looking at the spatial layout from four stationary viewing positions on the perimeter of the environment. Each child gave distance estimates among all pairs of landmarks. For the younger children, walking through the environment facilitated performance for the large-scale environment. Type of acquisition experience did not make a difference in performance when the navigable/small-scale space was involved. The distance estimates of the fifth-grade children were not differentially influenced by type of environment or type of acquisition experience.

Conclusions

Do the processing demands required for manipulation and/or representation of spatial information derived from the different kinds of environments discussed here differ or are they largely the same? This is the central question of this chapter and one that will be addressed more directly in this section. It is very difficult to make comparisons among the studies that have used spaces varying in scale and/or size because they vary in many other ways as well. Nonetheless, some general impressions can be drawn from these spatial cognition studies.

The comparison of greatest interest here is that between cognition/behavior in interactions with model spaces on the one hand and with the larger spaces (that is, navigable/small-scale and large-scale) on the other hand. The model spaces, of course, differ structurally from the navigable/small-scale spaces in terms of size and from the large-scale spaces in terms of both size and scale. A great deal of interest has been expressed in recent years over this microspace versus macrospace distinction (see, for example, Acredolo, 1977; Herman and Siegel, 1978; Weatherford and Cohen, 1980). This distinction is especially important because a model space is considered somewhat artificial and contrived, being a physical representation of a real world environment. Both types of large spaces, of course, are much more like the spaces we move through every day. Wayfinding and orientation occur in large, open spaces in which one can move freely and explore. Thus, it is reasonable to be concerned about generalizing from spatial behaviors observed in research using the tabletop model or microspaces to the larger, full-size spaces.

It may be helpful at this point to look at studies using model spaces to determine if they have produced findings similar to those studies that have employed the larger spaces. Let us first consider the perspective-taking research, mindful that very few perspective studies have been conducted in the larger spaces. Nevertheless, at least two general findings have been reported in research with each of the three types of environmental spaces. The first concerns a mental transformation of spatial information known as array rotation. Array rotation is essentially the converse of perspective-taking, since the subject is required to imagine a particular view of the environment given an imaginary rotation of the spatial layout itself. With a model space (for example, Harris and Bassett, 1976; Huttenlocher and Presson, 1973), a navigable/small-scale space (Herman and Coyne, 1980), and a large-scale space (Hardwick, McIntyre, and Pick, 1976), researchers have concluded that perspective taking is a more difficult conceptual transformation than array rotation. The second finding common to all three types of spaces is that perspective ability is a developmental phenomenon. Model studies demonstrating developmental improvement in this ability have been numerous (for example, Nigl and Fishbein, 1974; Piaget and Inhelder, 1967), and have been supported by findings in a navigable/small-scale space (Acredolo, 1977; Herman and Coyne, 1980), and a large-scale space (Hardwick, McIntyre, and Pick, 1976).

Similar findings produced in both small and large spaces concern array differentiation, locomotor movement, and shielding of the array. The fact that perspective coordination is easier for young children when the spatial layout contains differentiating cues relative to a situation with few such cues has been demonstrated in both a model space (see Borke, 1975; Pufall and Shaw, 1973; Shlechter and Salkind, 1979) and in a navigable/small-scale space (Acredolo, 1977). The facilitative role of locomotor movement on perspective taking has been demonstrated using a model space despite the fact that one cannot move around within the space. Studies by Huttenlocher and Presson (1973), Schatzow, Kahane, and Youniss (1980), and Shantz and Watson (1971) have all demonstrated that subjects' perspective taking can be enhanced if they are allowed to walk around the spatial array prior to making the perspective judgments. Weatherford and Cohen (1980) used a navigable/small-scale space to show that not only does movement influence perspective-taking accuracy but different patterns of movement can affect perspective judgments differently. Finally, a finding produced using a model space and corroborated in a full-size space is that egocentric responding can be reduced in a perspectives task if a shield is used to preclude the subject from viewing the spatial array during the judgments. Several model studies have demonstrated this (see, for example, Brodzinsky, Jackson, and Overton, 1972; Huttenlocher and Presson, 1973) and the same result was reported in a large-scale space study (Hardwick, McIntyre, and Pick, 1976).

As noted, few cognitive-mapping studies have been done on model arrays. Yet available evidence suggests that the representational mapping of model spaces can be influenced by factors in much the same way as mapping of the full-size spaces. For example, a microspatial layout has been used to show that certain patterns of movement (of a model train) can affect the representation that one constructs of the array of landmarks (Anooshian and Wilson, 1977). This is roughly similar to the finding that different kinds of movement influence different representations of navigable/small-scale spaces (see Herman, 1980) and large-scale spaces (Cohen and Weatherford, 1981; Hazen, Lockman, and Pick, 1978). Also, improved mapping performance has been shown to result from reliance upon an objective frame of reference in both a model space (Watkins and Schadler, 1980) and in a navigable/small-scale space (Acredolo, 1978).

One can be encouraged by how various findings about spatial behavior with models have been supported in the large space studies. At the very least, we can feel that model spaces are useful and allow us a better understanding of perspective taking and cognitive mapping and what can influence their execution and accuracy in real world situations. Still, we do not yet have the evidence to allow any firm conclusions about the comparability of the cognitive processes that underlie such phenomena as they are applied in microspatial and macrospatial situations. Given the present state of the art, we must be tentative in our generalizations from model spaces to full-size spaces and recognize that "the processes applied to the two spaces are not necessarily isomorphic" (Acredolo, 1977, p. 7).

Even if the mental processes that are applied in the two situations are similar, there are clearly limitations to the microspatial environments. One must always remain outside the model space, never experiencing the space from within as a participant. This inside/outside distinction has been presented as an important one in both theory (Ittelson, 1973) and research (see, for example, Herman, 1980; Weatherford and Cohen, 1980). Furthermore, it would be difficult to use a model space to examine the roles of variables such as familiarity, barriers, locomotion, and the socioemotional quality of environments.

Thus far in this section, only the distinction between the small, model space and the two kinds of large, full-size spaces has been considered. It is particularly important to question the ecological validity of the smaller spaces and determine if the spatiocognitive processes applied to these models are the same ones applied in the larger spaces. Also worthy of recognition is the distinction between the navigable/small-scale and the large-scale spaces.

Weatherford and Cohen (1981) point out the value of distinguishing between these two types of full-size spaces. Their comparison study shows that processing of spatial information from large spaces differing only in scale are not necessarily equivalent. This warns us against lumping all large spaces together as though one were just like another in terms of cognitive-mapping demands. It also demonstrates that the small-scale/large-scale dichotomy is not adequate to encompass all the different kinds of spaces. In fact, the trifold distinction made here is likely inadequate as well and could readily be dropped in favor of a well-developed view of the processing demands of space. If we can begin to determine that there are processing differences across various environments and what these differences are, then it may be beneficial to move our emphasis away from the structural aspects of the environment (for example, size, scale) toward viewing environments more directly in terms of the demands made on spatiocognitive processes. Thus, a model space, a navigable/small-scale space, and a large-scale space may differ not only in terms of size and scale but also along a continuum of cognitive demands.

In conclusion, it seems that spatial cognition researchers have been overexclusive in their descriptions of environments, generally specifying only structural features such as size, shape, and contents. In many instances, physical demands (for example, having to walk around barriers or up hills) and/or cognitive demands (for example, having to integrate numerous percepts) necessitated by the environment on an observer are not described. In addition, psychological aspects of environments such as meaningfulness, function, and familiarity are sometimes overlooked. Future efforts should include attempts to consider all of the physical and psychological features of the environment and how these may influence the observer's processing of spatial information.

References

Acredolo, L. P. "Developmental Changes in the Ability to Coordinate Perspectives of a Large-Scale Space." *Developmental Psychology,* 1977, *13,* 1–8.

16

References

Acredolo, L. P. "Developmental Changes in the Ability to Coordinate Perspectives of a Large-Scale Space." *Developmental Psychology,* 1977, *13,* 1–8.

Acredolo, L. P. "Development of Spatial Orientation in Infancy." *Developmental Psychology,* 1978, *14,* 224–234.

Acredolo, L. P. "Small- and Large-Scale Spatial Concepts in Infancy and Childhood." In L. Liben, A. Patterson, and N. Newcombe (Eds.), *Spatial Representation and Behavior Across the Life Span.* New York: Academic Press, 1981.

Acredolo, L. P., Pick, H. L., and Olsen, M. G. "Environmental Differentiation and Familiarity as Determinants of Children's Memory for Spatial Location." *Developmental Psychology,* 1975, *11,* 495–501.

Anooshian, L. J., and Wilson, K. L. "Distance Distortions in Memory for Spatial Locations." *Child Development,* 1977, *48,* 1704–1707.

Appleyard, D. "Styles and Methods of Structuring a City." *Environment and Behavior,* 1970, *2,* 100–118.

Borke, H. "Piaget's Mountains Revisited: Changes in the Egocentric Landscape." *Developmental Psychology,* 1975, *11,* 240–243.

Brodzinsky, D., Jackson, J., and Overton, W. "Effects of Perceptual Shielding in the Development of Spatial Perspectives." *Child Development,* 1972, *43,* 1041–1046.

Cohen, R., Baldwin, L. M., and Sherman, R. C. "Cognitive Maps of a Naturalistic Setting." *Child Development,* 1978, *49,* 1216–1218.

Cohen, R., and Weatherford, D. L. "Effects of Route Traveled on the Distance Estimates of Children and Adults." *Journal of Experimental Child Psychology,* 1980, *29,* 403–412.

Cohen, R., and Weatherford, D. L. "The Effect of Barriers on Spatial Representations." *Child Development,* 1981, *52,* 1087–1090.

Cohen, R., Weatherford, D. L., and Byrd, D. "Distance Estimates of Children as a Function of Acquisition and Response Activities." *Journal of Experimental Child Psychology,* 1980, *30,* 464–472.

Cohen, R., Weatherford, D. L., Lomenick, T., and Koeller, K. "Development of Spatial Representations: Role of Task Demands and Familiarity with the Environment." *Child Development,* 1979, *50,* 1257–1260.

Eliot, J., and Dayton, C. M. "Factors Affecting Accuracy of Perception on a Task Requiring the Ability to Identify Viewpoints." *Journal of Genetic Psychology,* 1976, *128,* 201–214.

Fehr, L. "Methodological Inconsistencies in the Measurement of Spatial Perspective-Taking Ability: A Cause for Concern." *Human Development,* 1978, *21,* 302–315.

Fehr, L. "Spatial Landmarks Revisited: Are They Useful?" *Journal of Genetic Psychology,* 1980, *136,* 299–300.

Feldman, A., and Acredolo, L. P. "The Effect of Active Versus Passive Exploration on Memory for Spatial Location in Children." *Child Development,* 1979, *50,* 698–704.

Fishbein, H., Lewis, S., and Keiffer, K. "Children's Understanding of Spatial Relations: Coordination of Perspectives." *Developmental Psychology,* 1972, *7,* 21–33.

Hardwick, D. A., McIntyre, C. W., and Pick, H. L. "The Content and Manipulation of Cognitive Maps in Children and Adults." *Monographs of the Society for Research in Child Development,* No. 166, 1976, *41* (entire issue).

Harris, P., and Bassett, E. "Reconstruction from the Mental Image." *Journal of Experimental Child Psychology,* 1976, *21,* 514–523.

Hazen, N. L., Lockman, J. J., and Pick, H. L. "The Development of Children's Representations of Large-Scale Environments." *Child Development,* 1978, *49,* 623–636.

Herman, J. F. "Children's Cognitive Maps of Large-Scale Spaces: Effects of Exploration, Direction, and Repeated Experience." *Journal of Experimental Child Psychology,* 1980, *29,* 126–143.

Herman, J. F., and Coyne, A. C. "Mental Manipulation of Spatial Information in Young and Elderly Adults." *Developmental Psychology,* 1980, *16,* 537–538.

Herman, J. F., and Siegel, A. W. "The Development of Cognitive Mapping of the Large-Scale Environment." *Journal of Experimental Child Psychology,* 1978, *26,* 389–406.

Hoy, E. "Predicting Another's Visual Perspective: A Unitary Skill?" *Developmental Psychology,* 1974, *10,* 462.

Huttenlocher, J., and Presson, C. "Mental Rotation and the Perspective Problem." *Cognitive Psychology,* 1973, *4,* 277–299.

Ittelson, W. H. "Environment Perception and Contemporary Perceptual Theory." In W. H. Ittelson (Ed.), *Environment and Cognition.* New York: Seminar Press, 1973.

Knudson, K., and Kagan, S. "Visual Perspective Role-Taking and Field-Independence Among Anglo-American and Mexican-American Children of Two Ages." *Journal of Genetic Psychology,* 1977, *131,* 243–253.

Kosslyn, S. M., Pick, H. L., and Fariello, G. R. "Cognitive Maps in Children and Men." *Child Development,* 1974, *45,* 707–716.

Ladd, F. C. "Black Youths View Their Environment: Neighborhood Maps." *Environment and Behavior,* 1970, *2,* 64–79.

Liben, L. "Perspective-Taking Skills in Young Children: Seeing the World Through Rose-Colored Glasses." *Developmental Psychology,* 1978, *14,* 87–92.

Miller, J. "Measuring Perspective Ability." *Journal of Geography,* 1967, *66,* 167–171.

Minnigerode, F., and Carey, R. "Development of Mechanisms Underlying Spatial Perspectives." *Child Development,* 1974, *45,* 496–498.

Nigl, A., and Fishbein, H. "Perception and Conception in Coordination of Perspectives." *Developmental Psychology,* 1974, *45,* 496–498.

Piaget, J., and Inhelder, B. *The Child's Conception of Space.* New York: Norton, 1967.

Piaget, J., Inhelder, B., and Szeminska, A. *The Child's Conception of Geometry.* New York: Basic Books, 1960.

Pufall, P., and Shaw, R. "Analysis of the Development of Children's Spatial Reference Systems." *Cognitive Psychology,* 1973, *5,* 151–175.

Salatas, H., and Flavell, J. "Perspective Taking: The Development of Two Components of Knowledge." *Child Development,* 1976, *47,* 103–109.

Schatzow, M., Kahane, D., and Youniss, J. "Effects of Movement on Perspective Taking and the Coordination of Perspectives." *Developmental Psychology,* 1980, *16,* 582–587.

Shantz, C. "The Development of Social Cognition." In E. M. Hetherington (Ed.), *Review of Child Development Research.* Vol. 5. Chicago: University of Chicago Press, 1975.

Shantz, C., and Watson, J. "Spatial Abilities and Spatial Egocentrism in the Young Child." *Child Development,* 1971, *42,* 171–181.

Shemyakin, F. N. "Orientation in Space." In B. G. Ananyev and others, (Eds.), *Psychological Science in the USSR.* Vol. 1, Part 1, No. 11466. Washington, D.C.: U.S. Office of Technical Reports, 1962.

Shlechter, T., and Salkind, N. "Influences of Environmental Differentiation and Conceptual Tempo on Young Children's Spatial Coordination." *Perceptual and Motor Skills,* 1979, *48,* 1091–1097.

Siegel, A. W. "The Externalization of Cognitive Maps by Children and Adults: In Search of Ways to Ask Better Questions." In L. S. Liben, A. H. Patterson, and N. Newcombe (Eds.), *Spatial Representations and Behavior Across the Life Span.* New York: Academic Press, 1981.

Siegel, A. W., Herman, J. F., Allen, G. L., and Kirasic, K. C. "The Development of Cognitive Maps of Large- and Small-Scale Space." *Child Development,* 1979, *50,* 582–585.

Siegel, A. W., and Schadler, M. "Young Children's Cognitive Maps of Their Classroom." *Child Development,* 1977, *48,* 388–394.

Watkins, B., and Schadler, M. "The Development of Strategy Use in a Spatial Task." *Journal of Genetic Psychology,* 1980, *137,* 109–117.

Weatherford, D. L., and Cohen, R. "Influence of Prior Activity on Perspective Taking." *Develomental Psychology,* 1980, *16,* 239–240.

Weatherford, D. L., and Cohen, R. "The Influence of Locomotor Activity on Spatial Representations of Large-Scale Environments." Paper presented at the biennial meeting of the Society for Research in Child Development, Boston, April 3, 1981.

David L. Weatherford is currently a postdoctoral fellow at the John F. Kennedy Center for Research on Education and Human Development, Vanderbilt University, Nashville, Tennessee.

Researchers frequently refer to the familiarity of an environment
when discussing a subject's performance on a spatial task.
But what exactly is familiarity, and how does it come about?

The Familiarity Factor in Spatial Research

Linda P. Acredolo

If one were to ask people on the street what one factor contributes most heavily to their ability to get around in their home city, my bet would be that nine times out of ten they would answer in one of two ways—either "I get around well *because* I'm very familiar with the city" or "I get around well because I've lived here a long time and *therefore* I'm familiar with the city." How do these two statements differ? The difference is subtle but important because it provides us with a framework for organizing the existing literature on the role of familiarity in spatial knowledge. The purpose of this chapter will be to present this framework, indicate briefly how existing studies fall within it, and finally describe a little recent data of my own in which the contribution of one rarely considered aspect of familiarity is demonstrated.

Back to the statements from our "man on the street." In the case of the first one ("I get around well *because* I'm very familiar with the city"), familiarity is being cited as a reason for, a cause of, good spatial knowledge of the environment. In psychological terms, familiarity in this instance is being viewed as an *independent* variable—that is, a variable that is responsible for change in dependent variables that can be measured, such as the ability to draw a map or to remember a spatial location. The existing literature has many examples of studies adopting this view of familiarity. One example is a study of my own (Acredolo, Pick, and Olsen, 1975). We assessed the child's ability to recall

R. Cohen (Ed.). *New Directions for Child Development: Children's Conceptions of Spatial Relationships*, no. 15.
San Francisco: Jossey-Bass, March 1982.

where a set of keys had been accidentally dropped when this event occurred in a familiar play area versus an unfamiliar office area.

Before we elaborate on this first view, let us compare it to a subtly different view, one illustrated clearly in the second statement by our "man on the street." In this case, the answer to our query is not "I get around well *because* I'm familiar with the city" but, rather, "I get around well because I've lived here a long time and *therefore* I'm very familiar with the city." What is illustrated here is the equating of familiarity with good spatial knowledge; familiarity *is* knowing one's way around. Furthermore, an underlying reason for, cause of, that familiarity/knowledge is being suggested. In this case, the presumed explanation is one frequently cited in the literature—that is, length of residence. The difference here in psychological terms is that familiarity is being treated as a *dependent* variable and the search is for the independent variables, such as length of residence, that cause familiarity to increase. The classic example in this case is Appleyard (1970), in which newcomers' familiarity with the layout of a city was compared to that of long-term residents through analysis of their sketch maps.

To review, the literature on familiarity can be divided into two categories: first, those studies treating familiarity as an independent variable and then searching for how knowledge changes as a function of increased familiarity; and, second, those studies treating familiarity as a dependent variable and then searching for the factors responsible for causing an increase in familiarity (viewed as synonymous with knowledge). One can summarize these two approaches quite easily. Those studies treating familiarity as an independent variable are asking, "What does familiarity breed?" and those studies treating familiarity as a dependent measure are asking, "What breeds familiarity?" Now let us look at each category more closely.

What Does Familiarity Breed?

The emphasis in studies within this category has been on describing milestones in the development of spatial knowledge from a microgenetic point of view. Questions asked often have to do, for example, with the role of landmarks versus paths in early versus later exposure to an environment, the degree of metric versus topological accuracy to be expected at various points in the familiarity timeline, or the impact of increased familiarity on one's emotional state or aesthetic appreciation of an environment.

Fortunately, a reassuring degree of consensus seems to be developing in the literature in regard to at least the first two of these questions. Therefore, the literature can be summarized relatively briefly. Both Siegel and his associates (Siegel, Kirasic, and Kail, 1978; Siegel and White, 1975;) and Golledge and his associates (Golledge and others, forthcoming) have concluded from their work and the work of others that knowledge of an environment begins with the noticing of landmarks (or *primary nodes,* in Golledge's terminology) that become linked in memory by action sequences called routes. These land-mark-route combinations form clusters, with knowledge of intracluster spatial relations proceeding much more quickly than between-cluster coordination. Indeed, it is the ability to properly coordinate separate clusters within a large-scale, objective frame of reference that marks the final step in the developmental process. Gary Allen, in this volume, discusses the work in this area. In addition to affecting better knowledge of the relative position of landmarks, increased familiarity also is thought to yield more accurate metric knowl-edge — what is often called in the literature "fine tuning." A number of excel-lent papers reviewing literature supportive of this model already exist (Evans, 1980; Siegel, Kirasic, and Kail, 1978; Siegel and White, 1975). Instead of duplicating their efforts here, let us move on to the other relevant question, "What breeds familiarity?"

What Breeds Familiarity?

The answer to this question is that a multitude of factors do. Since a thorough evaluation of the relevant research here would take more space than we have, let me simply outline some of the more salient factors that have received attention. When viewed as synonymous with knowledge, familiarity has been found to be a function of at least the following four factors: the amount of exposure to the environment, the type or quality of exposure, characteristics of the observer, and the nature of the environment itself.

Amount of Exposure. Although this factor is perhaps the first one to come to mind, it is often so confounded with other variables, such as the nature of the environment (for example, emotional significance), that its own contri-bution is difficult to assess. However, we do have evidence from both labora-tory and real-world environments that supports the importance of amount of exposure to spatial knowledge. In laboratory settings, amount of exposure is usually operationalized as the number of training trials during which the sub-ject is exposed to the environmental stimuli. Herman and Siegel (1978), for example, varied the number of trips children were allowed through a model village and found impressive degrees of improvement in memory for the lay-out of the village by seven- and ten-year-old children as the number of trips increased. Even five-year-olds showed improvement as long as topological information from the environment external to the experimental village was available (Experiment 1). Varying the number of times a trip is seen repre-sented in a series of slides is a second way in which amount of exposure is manipulated in the laboratory. Improvement with increased exposure has been noted here, particularly in the fine tuning of one's knowledge (Allen, Sie-gel, and Rosinski, 1978; Allen and others, 1979).

In large-scale environments outside of the laboratory, amount of expo-sure is usually operationalized in terms of length of residence. For example, Milgram and his associates (1972) found that residents of New York City could recognize photos of their own home borough better than photos of any other borough except Manhattan. Actually, the high level of recognition for Manhattan is also in part a function of amount of exposure, since the subjects reported visiting Manhattan frequently. However, we have here a good example of how amount of exposure can interact with other variables. Manhattan is not only frequently visited; it is also full of highly distinctive and emotionally significant landmarks, thus illustrating the importance of the nature of the environment to the familiarity issue.

How does one separate the effects of amount of exposure from the effects of other variables? A recent study by Sadalla, Burroughs, and Staplin (1980) illustrates one attempt. These researchers identified a number of landmarks on a university campus that were operating as reference points around which spatial knowledge of other landmarks and paths was being organized. They then asked subjects to rate these reference points on eighteen semantic differential scales designed to measure such things as cultural importance, visibility, size, and frequency of use. The results of the hierarchical cluster analysis revealed that the best predictor of whether a landmark was a reference point was its rating on the familiarity scale ($r = .84$). Other strong predictors were "dominates nearby places" ($r = .60$), "cultural importance" ($r = .48$), and "near the center of a region" ($r = .45$) — all measures dealing with the nature of the environment. How, then, does this pattern provide support for the "amount of exposure" argument? The support comes roundabout from the fact that the familiarity scale that predicted the reference points so strongly itself clustered most strongly with the "often used/rarely used" dimension. To these subjects, then, a judgment of familiarity was a judgment about the frequency of exposure.

Type of Exposure. We know that the specific way in which one experiences an environment affects one's knowledge of that environment. At least three subfactors have received attention in the literature. The most commonly cited of these is the effect of mode of travel, often also referred to as active-versus-passive dimension. Appleyard (1970) was one of the first to document that subjects who drove through their city were more knowledgeable about spatial information than those who rode public transportation. Since then, additional support from adult populations has been provided by Beck and Wood (1976), who also report that automobile drivers produce better sketch maps of a city than do pedestrians, with mass transit riders falling in between. One reason, they suggest, is because street signs tend to be positioned so that they fall more immediately within the visual field of the driver. Thus, the mode-of-travel factor probably influences the type of environmental information to which one attends. Modes of travel usually also differ both in the number of decisions that must be made and their geographic extent. Drivers, unlike mass transit riders, must continually make decisions about direction and, unlike pedestrians, generally must cover far greater geographical areas.

The impact of the mode-of-travel variable has also been demonstrated among young children. Feldman and Acredolo (1979), for example, had pre-schoolers and nine- and ten-year-olds walk through a complex of unfamiliar office hallways in search of a hidden object. Half the children at each age were accompanied by an adult holding their hand (passive condition), while the other half proceeded on their own with an adult following behind (active condition). After the object had been found and the walk completed, each child was asked to return to the location where the object had been found. The results indicated that the active exploration had significantly improved memory for the location among the preschoolers while not affecting the older children, who performed extremely well under either condition. Thus, it would seem that the traditional practice of holding on tightly to young children to prevent them from getting lost is actually somewhat counterproductive.

This conclusion is also supported by correlational data from Hazen (1979), who observed 1½- to 3½-year-old children and their parents in the naturalistic setting of a museum. As would be predicted from the Feldman and Acredolo (1979) study, the tendency for the child to lose his or her way in the museum was positively correlated ($r = .27$, $p < .05$) with parent-dependent movement and negatively correlated with independence scores ($r = -.32$, $p < 1$). Those children who were less likely to take the initiative in exploration were more likely to get lost. In a second phase of the study, Hazen found that children who spontaneously explored an artificial environment without heavy reliance on parental guidance performed better on a detour task and a route reversal task than children heavily dependent on such guidance, thus indicating the more independent children's sophisticated knowledge of the spatial layout. Of course, the correlational nature of these data leaves the question of causality unresolved. Perhaps skill at picking up spatial information leads to active exploration rather than the other way around. Fortunately, the experimental approach taken by Feldman and Acredolo (1979) provides some non-correlational evidence suggesting that mode of travel can indeed affect spatial knowledge at even these young ages.

Using an approach more similar to the adult literature, Hart (1979) compared the maps of children who were and were not bussed to school. The results indicated that the children who were bussed were much less likely to integrate the school's location with the location of their homes. In a thought-provoking discussion of the impact of school bussing, Lee (1963) extended this type of finding to the emotional realm by suggesting that the adjustment problems bussed children often show may at least in part be due to increased feelings of separation and isolation from home and the sense of security it symbolizes.

Finally, Benson and Uzgiris (1981) report that an active mode of travel is also helpful during infancy. In this case ten-month-old infants watched as an object was hidden under one of the two cloths within a large transparent box. They were then either carried to the opposite side to retrieve the object or allowed to crawl there on their own. The results indicated that the active mode resulted in significantly more accurate search than did the passive mode. Thus, it appears that the mode of travel variable is a powerful one whatever the age of the traveler. (See the chapter by Cohen in this volume for further discussion.)

However, the mode-of-travel/active versus passive dimension is not the only one relevant to the type-of-exposure issue. This category also includes a dimension commonly referred to as incidental versus intentional learning. Put quite simply, evidence indicates that if one is intentionally trying to learn the spatial layout of an environment, one is significantly more likely to be successful. The relevant research here comes from studies of both adults (Beck and Wood, 1976; Kozlowski and Bryant, 1977) and children (Acredolo, Pick, and Olsen, 1975). Kozlowski and Bryant (1977), for example, found that people reporting themselves to have a good sense of direction did no better at learning the spatial layout of an underground maze of tunnels than subjects not reporting such skill when neither group was aware that spatial knowledge would be tapped. When so informed, the subjects with the good sense of direction improved dramatically, while the subjects with the poor sense of direction did not. These results are important for two reasons. First, they indicate that keeping track of one's location in space is not automatic even for skilled individuals; it apparently requires conscious effort. Second, the study shows that the incidental-intentional aspect of the type-of-exposure factor interacts with subject variables, in this case the self-reported quality of one's sense of direction.

In an attempt to study the incidental-intentional factor developmentally, Acredolo, Pick, and Olsen (1975) took four- and eight-year-olds on a walk through an unfamiliar complex of office hallways. During the walk a set of keys was "accidentally" dropped. At the end of the walk, the children were asked to return to the site where the keys had been dropped. In the incidental condition, the children were unaware they would be required to locate the site, while, in the intentional condition, they were expecting to have to find the location again. The results were clear: Foreknowledge was helpful at each age. In addition, the same facilitative effect was found for the four-year-olds when the task was repeated in a familiar environment and in each environment regardless of the presence or absence of a salient landmark at the target location. Thus, it is clear that spatial knowledge—what I am calling familiarity—is in part a function of the conscious effort to retain spatial information and that this effect holds for children as young as three years of age.

A third variable falling within the type-of-exposure category involves the number of vantage points from which one views or experiences an environment. Evans and Pezdek (1980), for example, found that subjects who had learned a college campus from actual experience in the space were able to make judgments about the relative locations of buildings faster than were subjects who had learned the campus quite thoroughly but solely through viewing a map from a single vantage point. Subjects in the map condition apparently found it necessary to rotate their memory of the spatial relations in order to determine if their memory matched or did not match the relationship being presented. Such mental rotation was apparently unnecessary for subjects who had experienced the campus from many vantage points. Beck and Wood (1976) even suggest that it is actually the number-of-vantage-points dimension that accounts for the length-of-residence effect reported so frequently. Long-term residents, they argue, are much more likely to have experienced a city from multiple perspectives.

Characteristics of the Observer. So far we have focused on amount of exposure and type of exploration. What we have completely neglected is the nature of the observer. The fallacy of assuming that all individuals react the same way to the same environmental experience has been demonstrated in many ways. Clearly, the characteristic that has received the most attention is the age of the observer. Several excellent reviews of the developmental literature exist (Acredolo, 1981; Evans, 1980; Siegel, Kirasic, and Kail, 1978; Siegel and White, 1975), so I will not review the literature at length here. I would, however, like to make one point that others may have missed. My own research with infants as well as research by others (Acredolo, 1978, 1979; Acredolo and Evans, 1980; Bremner, 1978a, 1978b; Bremner and Bryant, 1977; Corter, Zucker, and Galligan, 1980; Rieser, 1979) suggests that frequency of exposure may have a different impact at these young ages than later in development. Specifically, if repeated exposure feeds an infant's tendency to organize space egocentrically, the result may be less accurate knowledge of the spatial environment. In other words, an infant who repeatedly views his mother entering the room from the right may come to expect her to enter from that direction even if the child's position in the room is suddenly altered. The number-of-vantage-points issue obviously becomes particularly important here as well.

Age, however, is not the only observer characteristic receiving attention. Kozlowski and Bryant (1977) provide evidence that individuals who judge themselves to have a good sense of direction are better able to learn a novel environment than individuals who perceive themselves to be poor at such tasks. A similar advantage was found by Thorndyke and Stasz (1980) for subjects with good visualization abilities. Such subjects were much better at learning information from maps than were subjects who scored poorly on a visualization pretest. Finally, Beck and Wood (1976) argue that individuals who have traveled extensively bring useful accumulated information about probable layouts of cities to each new environment. Such information facilitates learning of the new space. Beck and Wood also suggest that personality variables, such as whether one likes to travel in groups or on one's own, have an influence on spatial learning, although this effect is probably indirect and through the influence of factors like the active-passive dimension discussed earlier.

Nature of the Environment. The last major category that contributes to the breeding of familiarity includes factors related to the structure of the environment itself. Very briefly, important dimensions here include the redundancy of the layout (Beck and Wood, 1976), the degree to which the layout conforms to Gestalt laws of good perceptual organization (Kozlowski and Bryant, 1977; Peterson, 1916; Tversky, forthcoming), the presence of barriers and directness of routes (Anooshian and Wilson, 1977; Cohen, Baldwin, and Sherman, 1978; Cohen and Weatherford, 1980; Kosslyn, Pick, and Fariello, 1974), and the legibility, visibility, and significance of landmarks (Appleyard, 1969; Lynch, 1960; Milgram and others, 1972; Sadalla, Burroughs, and Staplin, 1980).

Affective Factors

Although it seems we surely must have exhausted the factors contributing to our two initial questions ("What does familiarity breed?" and "What breeds familiarity?"), one important dimension has been overlooked. A famous quotation from Lynch's 1960 classic, *The Image of the City*, illustrates it well: "To become completely lost is perhaps a rather rare experience for most people. . . . But let the mishap of disorientation once occur, and the sense of anxiety and even terror that accompanies it reveals to us how closely it is linked to our sense of balance and well-being" (p. 4). The point being illustrated here, of course, is that familiarity with an environment breeds not only more precise metric knowledge and better coordination of landmark clusters but also a sense of emotional security. While this is true enough, I would like to extend the argument even further to suggest that not only does familiarity breed security but that feelings of security also in turn breed familiarity. What I mean by this is quite simply that if one is highly aroused, one is considerably less likely to attend to the very spatial information that might make the environment more familiar.

To illustrate my point I would like to describe very briefly a recent study I completed with nine-month-old infants. The study to be described was designed specifically to augment the results of a report (Acredolo, 1979) indicating superior performance on a spatial task among infants tested in their homes compared to infants tested in two unfamiliar laboratory environments. The task used in both that study and the current study required nine-month-old infants to watch as a toy was hidden under one of two cloths on a table, one to the right of midline and one to the left. The infants were then *immediately* moved to the opposite side of the table and allowed to search for the toy. No attempt to search was allowed from the original position. Of interest was whether the infants would remember the correct location of the toy despite their movement to the opposite vantage point or whether they would instead disregard the movement and choose the cloth that maintained their original relationship with the toy. In other words, would their choice be objective or egocentric?

The results of the study (Acredolo, 1979) indicated quite clearly that environmental familiarity played a role: While 65 percent of the infants in each laboratory environment chose egocentrically, only 13 percent of those tested in their homes did so. But what exactly was it about the home environment that was influencing performance? Were the infants better oriented in the home? Were the objects in the home operating as landmarks? Or were the infants, perhaps, more secure in the home and consequently better able to attend to the task itself? The present study was specifically designed to evaluate this third, often overlooked, contribution of familiarity.

In contrast to the original study, which had included a typical, short, get-acquainted period prior to testing, the present procedure included a fifteen-minute play period specifically designed to maximize the infant's feelings of security in the experimental space itself. The space was the same ten-foot by ten-foot landmark-free enclosure used in the original study, thus ruling out any familiarity effect evolving from increased differentiation of spatial features. A shallow wading pool (to keep the child in one place) containing a variety of attractive toys was introduced into the space, and infant, mother, and experimenter interacted with one another for fifteen minutes. The pool was then removed, the task materials introduced, and the task completed.

The resulting change in performance from the original study was striking. Of the sixteen infants tested, thirteen chose one of the two cloths. Of these thirteen, only three (19 percent of the total N) chose egocentrically. This is a significant drop from the 65 percent found in the same environment without the extended pretask familiarization period ($p < .01$). Since familiarity in this case did not involve increased knowledge of landmarks, the results demonstrated the need to expand the concept of familiarity to include the impact of such emotional factors as increased feelings of security. These results, it should be noted, do not negate the value of laboratory research. After all, infants are constantly finding themselves in totally unfamiliar spaces and it *is* important for us to learn exactly what kinds of spatial behaviors can be expected under such novel circumstances. The results, however, do suggest we be very cautious about generalizations to other environments. Researchers, beware: The performance-competence distinction is alive and well in spatial cognition. Lynn Liben's chapter in this volume further emphasizes this distinction.

The study just described also illustrates my basic point: The feelings of security allowed the child to attend to the spatial information being presented in the task, much as security in a large-scale environment allows a traveler to learn more about the surrounding spatial layout. The result is even greater levels of familiarity.

Of course, anyone familiar with the attachment literature would not be completely surprised at these results. One of the main functions of an attachment figure, according to the ethological perspective (see, for example, Ainsworth and Bell, 1970; Bowlby, 1969), is to provide a secure "home base" from which the child can explore the environment. As Samuels (1980) has shown, the presence of an older sibling in addition to the mother can also make a difference. With a sibling present, two-year-old children were observed to move farther from their mother in a novel environment, cover more area, stay away longer, and spend more time manipulating distant objects. Moreover, these behaviors were not simply imitations of the sibling's behaviors; the toddlers showed a good deal of independence as well as imitative activity. Presumably, these activities provided increased knowledge of the environment — what I am calling familiarity.

Summary

In this review of the familiarity literature, I have tried to suggest that the existing studies are fairly conveniently divisible into two categories, those emphasizing familiarity as an independent variable and those emphasizing familiarity as a dependent variable. Both approaches have proven fruitful. In addition, I have tried to point out the role of emotional security, which is an often neglected aspect of familiarity. The relationship can be summarized in the following way: What does familiarity breed? Security. And what does this security breed? Increased levels of familiarity.

Given all this, where should we go from here? It seems to me that, although we have been quite successful in identifying factors that influence environmental learning, we have as yet little if any idea how all these separate dimensions interact. Given the complexity of human behavior in every other domain psychology has attempted to explain, it looks like such a goal will keep us busy for a long time to come.

References

Acredolo, L. P. "Development of Spatial Orientation in Infancy." *Developmental Psychology*, 1978, *14*, 224–234.

Acredolo, L. P. "Laboratory Versus Home: The Effect of Environment on the Nine-Month-Old Infant's Choice of Spatial Reference System." *Developmental Psychology*, 1979, *15*, 666–667.

Acredolo, L. P. "Small- and Large-Scale Spatial Concepts in Infancy and Childhood." In L. Liben, A. Patterson, and N. Newcombe (Eds.), *Spatial Representation and Behavior Across the Life Span.* New York: Academic Press, 1981.

Acredolo, L. P., and Evans, D. "Developmental Changes in the Effects of Landmarks on Infant Spatial Behavior." *Developmental Psychology*, 1980, *16*, 312–318.

Acredolo, L. P., Pick, H. L., and Olsen, M. "Environmental Differentiation and Familiarity as Determinants of Children's Memory for Spatial Location." *Developmental Psychology*, 1975, *11*, 495–501.

Ainsworth, M. D. S., and Bell, S. M. "Attachment, Exploration, and Separation: Illustrated by the Behavior of One-Year-Olds in a Strange Situation." *Child Development*, 1970, *41*, 49–67.

Allen, G., Kirasic, K. C., Siegel, A. W., and Herman, J. F. "Developmental Issues in Cognitive Mapping: The Selection and Utilization of Environmental Landmarks." *Child Development*, 1979, *50*, 1062–1070.

Allen, G. L., Siegel, A. W., and Rosinski, R. R. "The Role of Perceptual Context in Structuring Spatial Knowledge." *Journal of Experimental Psychology: Human Learning and Memory*, 1978, *4*, 617–630.

Anooshian, L. J., and Wilson, K. L. "Distance Distortions in Memory for Spatial Locations." *Child Development,* 1977, *48,* 1704-1707.

Appleyard, D. "Why Buildings Are Known." *Environment and Behavior,* 1969, *1,* 131-156.

Appleyard, D. "Styles and Methods of Structuring a City." *Environment and Behavior,* 1970, *2,* 100-116.

Beck, R. J., and Wood, D. "Cognitive Transformation of Information from Urban Geographic Fields to Mental Maps." *Environment and Behavior,* 1976, *8,* 199-238.

Benson, J. B., and Uzgiris, I. C. "The Role of Self-Produced Movement in Spatial Understanding." Paper presented at the biennial meeting of the Society of Research in Child Development, Boston, April 2, 1981.

Bowlby, J. *Attachment and Loss.* Vol. 1. *Attachment.* New York: Basic Books, 1969.

Bremner, J. G. "Egocentric Versus Allocentric Spatial Coding in Nine-Month-Old Infants: Factors Influencing the Choice of Code." *Developmental Psychology,* 1978a, *14,* 346-355.

Bremner, J. G. "Spatial Errors Made by Infants: Inadequate Spatial Cues for Evidence of Egocentrism." *British Journal of Psychology,* 1978b, *69,* 77-84.

Bremner, J. G., and Bryant, P. E. "Place Versus Response as the Basis of Spatial Errors Made by Young Children." *Journal of Experimental Child Psychology,* 1977, *23,* 162-171.

Cohen, R., Baldwin, L. M., and Sherman, R. C. "Cognitive Maps of a Naturalistic Setting." *Child Development,* 1978, *49,* 1216-1218.

Cohen, R., and Weatherford, D. L. "Effects of Route Traveled on Distance Estimates of Children and Adults." *Journal of Experimental Child Psychology,* 1980, *29,* 403-412.

Corter, C. M., Zucker, K. J., and Galligan, R. F. "Patterns in the Infant's Search for Mother During Brief Separation." *Developmental Psychology,* 1980, *10,* 62-69.

Evans, G. W. "Environmental Cognition." *Psychological Bulletin,* 1980, *88,* 259-287.

Evans, G. W., and Pezdek, K. "Cognitive Mapping: Knowledge of Real-World Distance and Location Information." *Journal of Experimental Psychology,* 1980, *6,* 13-24.

Feldman, A., and Acredolo, L. "The Effect of Active Versus Passive Exploration on Memory for Spatial Location in Children." *Child Development,* 1979, *50,* 698-704.

Golledge, R. G., Richardson, G. D., Rayner, J., and Parnicky, J. J. "Procedures for Defining and Analyzing Cognitive Maps of the Mildly and Moderately Mentally Retarded." In H. L. Pick and L. P. Acredolo (Eds.), *Spatial Orientation: Theory, Research, and Applications.* New York: Plenum, forthcoming.

Hart, R. *Children's Experience of Place.* New York: Irvington, 1979.

Hazen, N. "Young Children's Knowledge and Exploration of Large-Scale Spaces." Paper presented at the biennial meeting of the Society for Research in Child Development, San Francisco, March 1979.

Herman, J., and Siegel, A. W. "The Development of Cognitive Mapping of the Large-Scale Environment." *Journal of Experimental Child Psychology,* 1978, *26,* 389-406.

Kosslyn, S. M., Pick, H. L., and Fariello, G. R. "Cognitive Maps in Children and Men." *Child Development,* 1974, *45,* 707-716.

Kozlowski, L. T., and Bryant, K. H. "Sense of Direction, Spatial Orientation, and Cognitive Maps." *Journal of Experimental Psychology: Human Perception and Performance,* 1977, *3,* 590-598.

Lee, T. R. "On the Relation Between the School Journey and Social and Emotional Adjustment in Rural Infant Children." *British Journal of Educational Psychology,* 1963, *27,* 100.

Lynch, K. *The Image of the City.* Cambridge, Mass.: M.I.T. Press, 1960.

Milgram, S., Greenwald, J., Keesler, S., McKenna, W., and Waters, J. "A Psychological Map of New York City." *American Scientist,* 1972, *60,* 194-200.

Peterson, H. "Illusions of Directional Orientation." *The Journal of Philosophy, Psychology, and Scientific Methods,* 1916, *13,* 225-236.

Rieser, J. "Spatial Orientation of Six-Month-Old Infants." *Child Development,* 1979, *50,* 1078–1087.

Sadalla, E. K., Burroughs, W. J., and Staplin, L. J. "Reference Points in Spatial Cognition." *Journal of Experimental Psychology: Human Learning and Memory,* 1980, *6,* 516–528.

Samuels, H. "The Effect of an Older Sibling on Infant Locomotor Exploration of a New Environment." *Child Development,* 1980, *51,* 607–609.

Siegel, A. W., Kirasic, K. C., and Kail, R. V. "Stalking the Elusive Cognitive Map: The Development of Children's Representations of Geographic Space." In J. F. Wohlwill and I. Altman (Eds.), *Human Behavior and Environment.* Vol. 3. New York: Plenum, 1978.

Siegel, A. W., and White, S. "The Development of Spatial Representations of Large-Scale Environments." In H. W. Reese (Ed.), *Advances in Child Development and Behavior.* Vol. 10. New York: Academic Press, 1975.

Thorndyke, P. W., and Stasz, C. "Individual Differences in Procedures for Knowledge Acquisition from Maps." *Cognitive Psychology,* 1980, *12,* 137–175.

Tversky, B. "Distortions in Memory for Maps." *Cognitive Psychology,* 1981, *13,* 407–433.

Linda P. Acredolo is an associate professor of psychology at the Davis campus of the University of California. She continues to be actively involved in the study of the development of spatial cognition, particularly during infancy.

Advances in the study of how children and adults acquire knowledge
of large-scale environments also provide insight into the course of
cognitive development in general.

The Organization of
Route Knowledge

Gary L. Allen

Many data have been collected, analyzed, and published since the early 1970s, when Hart and Moore (1973), Pick (1972), and Siegel and White (1975) called the attention of developmental psychologists to the area of inquiry concerned with children's acquisition and utilization of macrospatial knowledge. The upsurge of research in this area has been motivated by a number of factors, including a desire to study common, ecologically valid phenomena, a growing interest in visual/spatial information processing, and a need to establish a solid empirical bridge between theoretical statements about cognitive development and real-world activities. In view of this increased research interest, an obvious question comes to mind. What do we know now that we did not know then? What progress has been made in the study of the development of macrospatial cognition?

Some relatively recent publications have included statements that "data gathering has lagged far behind theory building in the study of the development of spatial representations of large-scale environments" (Allen and others, 1979, p. 1062) and that "we still know little about how these spatial representations are constructed or organized or what developmental changes occur in the organization of this knowledge" (Hazen, Lockman, and Pick, 1978, p. 623). However, these are really statements of how far there remains to go rather than complaints about our not having gone anywhere thus far. Indeed, we do

R. Cohen (Ed.). *New Directions for Child Development: Children's Conceptions of Spatial Relationships*, no. 15.
San Francisco: Jossey-Bass, March 1982.

know more about the development of spatial cognition now than we did in the early 1970s. Each of the contributions to this volume attests to this fact.

A Focus on Route Knowledge

The focus of this chapter is on route learning or, more specifically, on how route knowledge is organized. Simply stated, route learning involves acquiring information about the temporal and spatial relationships among environmental features; it is essentially a matter of sequence learning. Route learning may be regarded as an example of perceptual learning as Gibson (1969) used that term. As an individual acquires knowledge of the temporal and spatial relationships among environmental features along a route, he or she learns to differentiate among parts of the environment. Learning a route involves becoming "unconfused" about the spatial relationships among features along that route.

A distinction is often drawn between route learning and the acquisition of configurational (Siegel and White, 1975) or survey-type (Shemyakin, 1962) knowledge. Learning the layout of a large-scale spatial configuration requires the intercoordination of spatial relationships among a set of environmental features stripped of the temporal dimension. Because of the size and structure of large-scale environments, this intercoordination depends on an individual's ability to infer the locations of environmental features within a superordinate frame of reference. Once a set of spatial relationships has been established, as in the case of a city, it is possible to invent shortcuts or negotiate detours. Making logical inferences is a sophisticated process that improves dramatically during the cognitive growth of middle childhood (Piaget, 1970). Thus, it is not surprising that substantial development improvement has been predicted (Hart and Moore, 1973; Siegel, Kirasic, and Kail, 1978) and found (Curtis, Siegel, and Furlong, 1981; Hazen, Lockman, and Pick, 1978) in children's acquisition of configurational knowledge.

Emphasis on the development of configurational knowledge, however, has occasionally diverted researchers' attention from issues concerned with the development of route knowledge, which is a more fundamental form of spatial representation. Evidence from a variety of sources indicates that route learning is equally formidable as a focus for developmental inquiry. It has long been established that the ability to make use of distinctive visual features among stimuli improves over childhood (Gibson, 1969) and recent studies have demonstrated that visual search efficiency (Bisanz and Resnick, 1978) and recognition memory (Mandler and Robinson, 1978) improve developmentally. Logically, these processes play a part in route learning. Consequently, improvement in them leads to the expectation that route learning should also become more effective over childhood. In addition, Brown's (1976) studies of the child's construction of temporal sequences indicates that the cognitive components of route learning undergo important developmental changes. The chapter by Cohen in this volume as well as the work that will be described in this chapter bear out the expectations raised by these studies. The fact of ontogenetic improvement in route learning in and of itself is not unexpected. What is particularly noteworthy, however, is the way in which such demonstrated developmental change complements our understanding of cognitive development in general.

Empirical Studies

What follows is a description of two series of studies that serve to illustrate the links between research findings in macrospatial cognition and theoretical constructs in cognitive development. The first series, later referred to as *landmark studies,* concerns developmental differences in the selection and utilization of environmental landmarks. The second series, later referred to as *subdivision studies,* focuses on the role of subdivision, or segments, in organizing route knowledge. Both of these phenomena were studied using a procedure that involved first having participants in the experiments view a slide presentation depicting routes through real-world neighborhoods and then eliciting from these individuals proximity judgments involving features along the routes. The studies to be described were cross-sectional in design, involving groups of seven-year-olds, ten-year-olds, and college-age adults.

Landmark Studies. It was evident from other studies that both children and adults refer to environmental features when learning new surroundings, but it was not known whether children and adults tend to select the same features as reference points or whether children are able to discriminate among environmental features with regard to their potential landmark value in determining spatial relationships. A series of studies was designed to address these issues. In the first study, subjects at each of the three age levels selected scenes from a pictorialized walk that they considered to be high in potential landmark value — that is, those scenes that would serve as the best reminders of where one was along the walk. In the second study, other subjects at each age level were tested in a distance-ranking task in which the nine scenes most frequently selected by same-age peers were used as reference scenes. In addition, still other groups of seven- and ten-year-olds were tested with scenes selected by the adults.

The results of these studies were as follows. In selecting reference scenes, there was not much agreement across groups as to which were the highest in potential landmark value, although both intergroup and intragroup agreement increased slightly with age. Adults tended to select scenes depicting actual or potential changes in heading as being high in potential landmark value; intersections were in most of these photographs. Ten-year-olds selected fewer of these scenes than did college students, and the seven-year-olds selected even fewer. Instead, children tended to select scenes containing noticeable but spatially indeterminate features such as window displays and awnings, both of which were numerous along the walk. The nine most frequently selected scenes at each age level were identified for use in the second study. Overall, the seven- and ten-year-olds agreed with college students on two and four of the nine most frequently selected scenes, respectively.

Did these age-related differences indicate a developmental trend toward greater understanding of what environmental features are useful for spatial cues, or did they reflect disagreement among age groups with regard to landmark selection without implications for potential value as reference points? The results of the distance-ranking task suggest the former. In this task, subjects rank ordered the remaining eight scenes in terms of increasing distance, using each of the nine test scenes in turn as a point of origin. The accuracy of the resulting rank order data was determined through a combination of multidimensional scaling procedures. It was found that the performance of seven-year-olds in this task was not significantly affected by which set of reference scenes was used in testing. In other words, scenes selected by other seven-year-olds and those selected by adults as being high in potential landmark value yielded similarly low levels of accuracy. In contrast, the performance of ten-year-olds was significantly affected by this variable. When tested with scenes selected by their age peers, ten-year-olds performed no more accurately than did the seven-year-olds. However, when tested with scenes selected by adults, a group of ten-year-olds ranked distances with considerable accuracy. In fact, their performance was comparable to that of adults using the same photographs.

In summary, these studies indicate that (1) adults and children do not spontaneously select the same environmental features as reference points after viewing a route; (2) college students exhibit more accurate spatial knowledge of the route than do seven- or ten-year-old children when all subjects are tested with scenes selected by their age peers on the basis of potential landmark value; and (3) the older children, but not the younger children, reflect more accurate spatial knowledge of the route when tested with reference scenes selected by their age peers (Allen and others, 1979). This pattern of results suggests that the ability to make use of the potential landmark value of environmental features precedes developmentally the ability to select features on the basis of this potential information value.

As alluded to earlier, the significance of these findings is due in large part to the fact that they form an empirical link between the specialized area of macrospatial cognition and the broader field of cognitive development as a whole. In this case, the link is provided by the concepts of *evocation* and *utilization,* terms introduced a decade ago in Flavell's (1970) discussion of children's use of mnemonics. The failure to select scenes depicting the most useful spatial cues may be interpreted as a problem of evocation or, as it is sometimes expressed, a production deficiency. The failure to make use of spatial cues in the distance-judgment task may be considered a problem in utilization — that is, a mediation deficiency. According to this interpretation, seven-year-olds in this study exhibit both production and mediation deficiencies; they neither select scenes with high landmark value nor use such scenes when provided to increase the accuracy of their judgments. In contrast, ten-year-olds seem to have trouble only in selecting scenes containing good distance cues, not in using such scenes when provided. This pattern is compatible with what we know about memory development in a variety of other contexts. It seems reasonable to conclude that the selection and utilization of environmental landmarks embodies a mnemonic for learning real-world routes and, as in the case of other memory strategies, these skills improve developmentally in an orderly fashion. Children do learn about route learning itself. With experience, they learn which environmental features afford useful, low-effort spatial information and which do not.

Subdivision Studies. A second series of studies concerned the organization of route knowledge, with particular emphasis on how children and adults conceive of distance relations. Let us suppose that for the sake of cognitive efficiency, the continuous flow of perceptual information experienced by an individual traveling a route is "chunked" or organized into spatial segments, the boundaries of which are determined by simple topological concepts such as similarity, enclosure, and "belongingness." What would be the consequences of this organization scheme with regard to conceiving of distance relations? Previous research has shown that when an area is partitioned by artificial barriers in the lab (Kosslyn, Pick, and Fariello, 1974) or by environmental features in natural settings (Cohen, Baldwin, and Sherman, 1978), children and adults tend to exaggerate distances between separated regions. Despite this overall tendency, however, there is no question that the accuracy of distance judgments improves developmentally (Allen and others, 1979; Cohen, Weatherford, and Byrd, 1980). If the subdivision phenomenon is a reliable one, what is the nature of its effect on the accuracy of distance judgments in children and adults?

Two studies were conducted to begin answering this question. In the first study, groups of seven-year-olds, ten-year-olds, and college-age adults partitioned or subdivided a pictorialized route into segments. Scenes from the route were then used to create three types of proximity problems to be used in the second study. Each proximity problem consisted of three scenes from the walk, one serving as a reference scene and the other two as comparison scenes. The subject's task was to indicate which of the two comparison scenes was nearer the reference scene in terms of walking distance along the route. The three types of problems were as follows: (1) intrasubdivisional problems in which all three test scenes were in the same subdivision of the route; (2) intersubdivisional problems in which the distance from the reference scene to a comparison scene in an adjacent subdivision was less than the distance from the reference scene to the comparison scene within the same subdivision; and (3) intersubdivisional problems in which the distance from the reference scene to the comparison scene within the same subdivision was less than the distance from the reference scene to the comparison scene across the subdivision boundary.

It may be easier to illustrate these problem types using a neighborhood analogy. Type 1 would involve one standpoint and two locations all in the same neighborhood. Type 2 would involve a standpoint in one neighborhood that is actually closer to a standpoint in an adjacent neighborhood than to a location in the same neighborhood. Type 3 would involve a standpoint that is closer to a location in the same neighborhood than to a location in an adjacent neighborhood. In the experiment, easy and difficult distance discriminations were included for each type of problem, with easy discriminations involving a shorter-to-longer distance ratio of 1:3 (for example, 20m versus 60m) and difficult discriminations involving a 1:1.5 ratio (20m versus 30m). As in the initial study, seven-year-olds, ten-year-olds, and college-age adults were tested using these problems.

In the first study, considerable agreement was found both between and among age groups with regard to the boundaries of different route subdivisions. This agreement permitted the use of the same proximity problems for all groups in the second study. The results of that study were fairly straightforward. For intrasubdivisional problems, there was evidence of significant developmental improvement in terms of proportion of problems solved correctly. However, there was no such improvement for intersubdivisional problems. Subjects at all age levels tended to select the scene within the same subdivision as the one closer to the reference scene, even when this choice was metrically incorrect. In addition, the ratio of the two distances involved in the problems affected the difficulty of the intrasubdivisional problems only. In other words, the 1:3 and 1:1.5 ratio problems were easy and difficult, respectively, only when both distances were within the same subdivision. The ratio factor did not affect the accuracy with which intersubdivisional problems were solved. Furthermore, the distance ratio effect was in evidence for the ten-year-olds and college students on these intrasubdivisional problems but not for the seven-year-olds.

These findings serve to illustrate an important principle in cognitive development—namely, the emergence of redundant systems. Development is often conceived of in terms of more sophisticated processes replacing or superseding more primitive ones. However, it is sometimes the case that more sophisticated processes emerge to coexist with those that are more rudimentary. The advantage of such redundancy is greater flexibility in terms of matching task demands with appropriate effort.

In the study just described, developmental improvement in the overall accuracy of proximity judgments is not the result of a more sophisticated process based on subdivision judgments. Instead, the improvement reflects the emergence of a supplementary process based on the concept of metric distance. The supplemental status of the newer process is suggested by the fact that individuals who are capable of the more advanced process still rely consistently on subdivision designation for judging proximity when both means are available. In other words, when subdivision designation is available as a means of determining which of two scenes is closer to the reference point, both children and adults consistently rely on that information. In those instances in which a subdivisionally based judgment runs contrary to metric distances (that is, when the nearer scene is actually across a subdivision boundary), accuracy is traded for a savings in effort. However, when subdivision information is not sufficient for arriving at an answer to a proximity problem, as in the case of intrasubdivisional problems, the older subjects apply the additional effort and rely on their estimation ability while the younger children engage in guessing (Allen, 1981).

The Significance of Routes

At the conclusion of this chapter, it seems appropriate to reiterate that these studies of route representations and others concerned with the acquisition and utilization of spatial knowledge have implications beyond macrospatial cognition in and of itself. As reported earlier, interest in the study of macrospatial cognition has never been greater. This interest is attributable in part to an increased appreciation of the view that spatial thinking is in a real sense very basic or fundamental. This view abounds in heuristic implications. If macrospatial cognition is considered a simple, primitive form of human information processing, then it may serve as a useful model for more complex cognitive phenomena; by studying spatial cognition, investigators may gain valuable insight into other thought processes. At the very least, spatial metaphors are useful in describing complex relations between structure and process. In this regard, it is interesting to note the importance of spatial properties in, for example, theories of semantic memory (see, for example, Collins and Loftus, 1975). However, it is important to emphasize that the "basicness" of spatial cognition is of use to all of us in our everyday activities. Spatial concepts and properties of situations are often used in attempting to understand, remember, or communicate information.

How does route knowledge fit into this discussion? Route knowledge is an example of a linear mode of information representation. Its linearity is reflected in a temporospatial ordering of environmental features. Linearly organized information representations play an important role in cognitive activities as mnemonics and as problem-solving aids. A brilliant illustration of naturally occurring linear orders serving as mnemonic devices is provided by Luria (1968) in *The Mind of the Mnemonist.* Luria describes how one individual manifested extraordinary list-learning ability by cognitively distributing images of the items to-be-remembered in various places along a familiar route. In this case, the mnemonist used the method of loci — a well-known method for remembering a series of items — with unusual effectiveness (Siegel and White, 1975). An example of linear orders as problem-solving aids is provided by research into the solution of transitive inference problems (see Trabasso, 1977). Generically speaking, solving a transitive inference problem correctly requires that the relationship $A < C$ be inferred, given the information that $A < B$ and $B < C$. The number of items in the problem and the nature of the relationship to be inferred are variables. Evidence suggests that individuals are aided in solving these problems by internally representing them in a spatial mode (Trabasso, Riley, and Wilson, 1975).

These selected examples are not isolated cases. Just a moment's reflection reveals that many of the child's first tasks in a school setting involve learning and manipulating linear orders, including learning the alphabet and acquiring the concept of a number line. Even before these early school tasks are undertaken, however, children have had implicit experiences with linear orders in the sense that they have knowledge of familiar routes. To what extent children's spatial experience can be exploited in the service of education has yet to be examined. Nevertheless, it is useful to emphasize that the study of how route knowledge is acquired, organized, and utilized affords an avenue of inquiry that extends well beyond the horizon of macrospatial cognition as a specialized research area.

References

Allen, G. L. "A Developmental Perspective on the Effects of 'Subdividing' Macrospatial Experience." *Journal of Experimental Psychology: Human Learning and Memory*, 1981, *7*, 120–132.

Allen, G. L., Kirasic, K. C., Siegel, A. W., and Herman, J. F. "Developmental Issues in Cognitive Mapping: The Selection and Utilization of Environmental Landmarks." *Child Development*, 1979, *50*, 1062–1070.

Bisanz, J., and Resnick, L. B. "Changes with Age in Two Components of Visual Search Speed." *Journal of Experimental Child Psychology*, 1978, *25*, 129–142.

Brown, A. L. "The Construction of Temporal Succession by Preoperational Children." In A. D. Pick (Ed.), *Minnesota Symposia on Child Psychology*. Vol. 10. Minneapolis: University of Minnesota Press, 1976.

Cohen, R., Baldwin, L. M., and Sherman, R. C. "Cognitive Maps of a Naturalistic Setting." *Child Development*, 1978, *49*, 1216–1218.

Cohen, R., Weatherford, D. L., and Byrd, D. "Distance Estimates of Children as a Function of Acquisition and Response Activities." *Journal of Experimental Child Psychology*, 1980, *30*, 464–472.

Collins, A. M., and Loftus, E. F. "A Spreading-Activation Theory of Semantic Processing." *Psychological Review*, 1975, *82*, 407–428.

Curtis, L. E., Siegel, A. W., and Furlong, N. E. "Developmental Differences in Cognitive Mapping: Configurational Knowledge of Familiar Large-Scale Environments." *Journal of Experimental Child Psychology*, 1981, *31*, 456–469.

Flavell, J. H. "Developmental Studies of Mediated Memory." In H. W. Reese and L. P. Lipsitt (Eds.), *Advances in Child Development and Behavior*. Vol. 5. New York: Academic Press, 1970.

Gibson, E. J. *Principles of Perceptual Learning and Development*. New York: Appleton-Century-Crofts, 1969.

Hart, R. A., and Moore, G. T. "The Development of Spatial Cognition: A Review." In R. M. Downs and D. Stea (Eds.), *Image and Environment*. Chicago: Aldine, 1973.

Hazen, N. L., Lockman, J. J., and Pick, H. L. "The Development of Children's Representations of Large-Scale Environments." *Child Development,* 1978, *49,* 623–636.

Kosslyn, S. M., Pick, H. L., and Fariello, G. R. "Cognitive Maps in Children and Men." *Child Development,* 1974, *45,* 707–716.

Luria, A. R. *The Mind of a Mnemonist.* New York: Basic Books, 1968.

Mandler, J. M., and Robinson, C. A. "Developmental Changes in Picture Recognition." *Journal of Experimental Child Psychology,* 1978, *16,* 122–136.

Piaget, J. *Genetic Epistemology.* New York: Columbia University Press, 1970.

Piaget, J., and Inhelder, B. *The Child's Conception of Space.* New York: Norton, 1967.

Pick, H. L. "Mapping Children—Mapping Space." Presented at annual meetings of the American Psychological Association, Honolulu, September 1972.

Shemyakin, F. N. "Orientation in Space." In B. G. Ananyev (Ed.), *Psychological Science in the USSR.* Vol. 1, Part 1, No. 11466. Washington, D.C.: U.S. Office of Technical Reports, 1962.

Siegel, A. W., Kirasic, K. C., and Kail, R. V. "Stalking the Elusive Cognitive Map: The Development of Children's Representations of Geographic Space." In J. F. Wohlwill and I. Altman (Eds.), *Human Behavior and Environment.* Vol. 3. New York: Plenum, 1978.

Siegel, A. W., and White, S. H. "The Development of Spatial Representations of Large-Scale Environments." In H. W. Reese (Ed.), *Advances in Child Development and Behavior.* Vol. 10. New York: Academic Press, 1975.

Trabasso, T. T. "The Role of Memory as a System in Making Transitive Inferences." In R. V. Kail and J. W. Hagen (Eds.), *Perspectives on the Development of Memory and Cognition.* Hillsdale, N.J.: Erlbaum, 1977.

Trabasso, R., Riley, C. A., and Wilson, E. G. "The Representation of Linear Order and Spatial Strategies in Reasoning: A Developmental Study." In R. Falmagne (Ed.), *Reasoning: Representation and Process in Children and Adults.* Hillsdale, N.J.: Erlbaum, 1975.

Gary L. Allen is research assistant professor of psychology at Old Dominion University in Norfolk, Virginia.

Knowing your way around the environment involves more than just walking from here to there.

The Role of Activity in the Construction of Spatial Representations

Robert Cohen

Children and adults are able to move successfully among locations that are not directly perceivable from their current spatial position. Homes of friends are visited; routes to schools, shopping areas, offices, and so forth are negotiated. As noted by Siegel, Kirasic, and Kail (1978), researchers in the field of large-scale spatial cognition assume that our functioning in space is guided by an internal representation of that space. Since in large-scale environments all parts of the space cannot be viewed from a single vantage point, the individual is required to coordinate and integrate successive percepts in order to construct this internal, spatial representation. A second assumption is that the nature and applications of these spatial representations undergo developmental change. The cognitive ability of the individual, the type and amount of experience, and the social-affective milieu of settings all relate to these changes. The chapters in this volume examine critical contemporary issues in the field of the development of large-scale spatial cognition. The goal of the present chapter is to provide an analysis of the role of activity in space for the construction of spatial representations.

By their very nature, large-scale environments surround the individual, thus placing him or her in the role of participant within, as well as observer

R. Cohen (Ed.). *New Directions for Child Development: Children's Conceptions of Spatial Relationships,* no. 15. San Francisco: Jossey-Bass, March 1982.

of, the environment (Ittelson, 1973; see also the chapter by Weatherford in this volume). People move in space and, as noted above, multiple views are required in order to fully apprehend a large-scale environment. The nature and extent of activities that bring people into contact with these multiple views should influence the nature of the representation derived.

Walking has been the activity in space most often discussed. In fact, Siegel and White (1975) noted that, from a variety of theoretical perspectives, actual locomotion is assumed to be a critical condition for the construction of spatial representations. Walking provides direct sensorimotor information concerning spatial landmarks and actual or potential routes, both of which are presumed to be critical organizational features of spatial representations (Siegel and White, 1975).

It should be emphasized that a spatial representation is not a veridical copy or even maplike depiction of the environment. Psychological space is not isomorphic to physical space. For example, a shopping area in the downtown section of a city, although the same distance from residences as a more peripheral shopping area, is often believed by the residents to be closer to their homes (Lee, 1970). Spatial representations are constructed from experience. This construction is influenced by the nature of the experiences and by the cognitive status of the person.

The remainder of this chapter is devoted to an examination of the role of activity for the construction of spatial representations of children and adults. The focus of this presentation will be our program of research on the topic. The reader is directed to Siegel and White (1975) and Liben, Patterson, and Newcombe (1981) for related background information.

The Role of Activity

Our interest and research in the role of activity for the construction of spatial representations stem from two early studies. The first (Kosslyn, Pick, and Fariello, 1974) employed an experimental environment seventeen feet square. The environment contained ten stimulus locations and two sets of barriers that divided the space into quadrants. One set of barriers was large and opaque, thus preventing movement and viewing across quadrants. The other set of barriers was low, preventing movement but not inhibiting viewing across quadrants. Preschoolers and adults learned the placement of the stimulus locations by carrying objects from a home base to the location designated for the object in the space. Distance estimates were derived by having subjects rank order the closeness of objects and submitting the rank orderings to a multidimensional scaling computer analysis. Analysis of these derived distance estimates revealed that both preschoolers and adults overestimated the distance between objects separated by an opaque barrier. Only the preschoolers overestimated the distance between objects separated by a low, transparent barrier. Kosslyn, Pick, and Fariello (1974) suggested that young children are more influenced by functional distance considerations than are adults. That is, children base their judgments of physical distance on the actual walking distance between locations. Adults are able to compensate for necessary circuitous walking when visual information concerning physical distance is available.

Our first project in the area (Cohen, Baldwin, and Sherman, 1978) was conducted at a residential boys' camp in western Massachusetts. After having lived at the camp for one month, nine- and ten-year-old campers and adult counselors were asked to give estimates of distance among ten very familiar locations in the setting. The data were analyzed to determine the effects of barriers (buildings and/or trees) and hills in the environment on these distance estimates. Under certain response conditions, the presence of barriers led to overestimations of distance between locations. Thus the distortion due to barriers found by Kosslyn, Pick, and Fariello (1974) in an experimental environment was replicated here for a naturalistic setting. In addition, overestimations of distance resulted for locations with an intervening hill. It appears, then, that functional distance considerations involve more than just the length of a path walked; in addition, the effort required to negotiate a path enters into psychological considerations of physical distance.

These two studies demonstrate the cognitive construction of spatial representations. There is not an isomorphic mapping of the physical environment into a cognitive representation. Features of the environment and the cognitive status of the individual influence the process.

Relevant to the theme of the present chapter, there is a serious shortcoming in the studies by both Kosslyn, Pick, and Fariello (1974) and Cohen, Baldwin, and Sherman (1978). In neither were the paths walked by subjects controlled or assessed. Children and adults roamed relatively freely about the room while learning the arrangement of objects in Kosslyn, Pick, and Fariello (1974) and while at the summer camp in Cohen, Baldwin, and Sherman (1978). Thus it is impossible to determine the effects of actually walking specific paths between locations versus merely viewing the expanse between other locations. As noted previously, walking is presumed important in that it brings the individual into contact with the multiple views necessitated by a large-scale environment and thus facilitates the integration of these views.

Our next project (Cohen and Weatherford, 1980) was specifically designed to address the issue of the influence of walking some paths and not others on subsequent spatial representations. Second- and sixth-graders and college students were individually led through an experimental environment constructed in a large room. The environment consisted of seven stimulus locations and three large barriers. Each subject was led along a prescribed path, guessing the color of a card hidden at each location. The path was designed so that twelve of the twenty-one total pairwise interlocation distances represented the factorial combination of walked versus not walked, barrier-present versus barrier-absent, and length of interlocation distance (four, six, or eight feet). Following this acquisition experience, the subject was taken to an adjacent empty room of approximately the same dimensions as the experimental room. The subject was given color cards two at a time and told to place them on the floor so that they marked the actual distance between the locations designated by those color cards in the original environment. The individual was allowed to use any portion of the test room for this distance-estimation task.

The presence of barriers again led to overestimations of distance relative to barrier-free route estimates. Interestingly, however, estimates by all age groups were more accurate on barrier-present paths that were directly walked than on barrier-present paths that were never walked directly but were merely viewed. This experiment clearly demonstrates the complexity of the process of the construction of spatial representations and the limitation of functional distance as an explanation for environmentally produced distortions in those representations. Barrier-obstructed paths that were walked might have enhanced functional distance considerations; subjects might have monitored the effort and distance involved to move from one location to another. However, the sensorimotor information enhanced the accuracy of the representation rather than increasing distortion. These children and adults were able to take this information and compensate for the imposed circuitous travel when making physical distance estimates.

We have recently replicated this facilitative function of walking when barriers prohibit direct travel using a different task and a different environmental configuration (Cohen and Weatherford, 1981). In this experiment, we also varied the amount of experience in the environment and the type of experience (in terms of number of different paths actually walked). It appears that the actual number of different paths walked is unimportant when one has an optimal amount of time in the environment. When the time spent in the environment is limited, children have a more accurate representation of the environment when that time is spent on a small number of different paths than having that same amount of time distributed among a large number of different paths. Thus the time allotted for coordinating environmental perspectives interacts with the number of different perspectives one is required to coordinate. It is important to stress that this interaction occurred primarily on barrier-present paths that the individual was not allowed to walk directly.

The next step in our research program was to test the limits of the role of walking for the construction of spatial representations (Cohen, Weatherford, and Byrd, 1980). Second- and sixth-graders either actively walked about an experimental environment or stood passively on the perimeter of the environment and labeled the locations. In conjunction with these active versus passive acquisition conditions, the child performed subsequent interlocation distance estimates either actively or passively in an empty test room. That is, some children placed a color card (representing one location) at a start position and walked in a single direction to place a second card (active response); the remainder placed a color card at the start position and told the experimenter where to place the second card as the experimenter slowly backed away from the child along the single estimation direction (passive response). All pairwise interlocation estimates were performed one at a time, according to one of these response conditions.

Sixth-graders were equally accurate for all four combinations of acquisition and response activities. Second-graders were significantly more accurate when the acquisition and response activities were congruent (that is, active acquisition with active response, passive acquisition with passive response) than when the acquisition activity was passive and the response activity was active. Thus both acquisition and response activities affect performance on spatial tasks and influence interpretations concerning underlying spatial representations. Young children seem to be more influenced by the congruence between these conditions than older children. They perform better when required to use an activity similar to the one used when acquiring the information.

The issue of acquisition and response congruence was also examined by Siegel and others (1979). Kindergarteners and second- and fifth-graders learned the locations for either a small-scale or large-scale environment, then reconstructed the environment in either a small- or large-scale empty space. Children were more accurate when acquisition scale and response scale were congruent (that is, small-scale acquisition with small-scale response, large-scale acquisition with large-scale response) than when the scale of the acquisition environment was small and the response scale was large. Thus the match between how information is acquired and how it is retrieved is an important issue for young children. Siegel and his colleagues (1979) showed this with scale of environment; we demonstrated this with activity (Cohen, Weatherford, and Byrd, 1980).

It is difficult to summarize succinctly the experimental research on the influence of walking for the construction of spatial representations. Some research shows a facilitative effect for walking (Cohen and Weatherford, 1980, 1981); some shows no benefit relative to more passive activities (Cohen, Weatherford, and Byrd, 1980; Herman and Siegel, 1978). Self-directed movement aided young children in one study (Feldman and Acredolo, 1979) but not in another (Herman, 1980). These contradictory findings are due in part to three sources of variance among the studies: the operational definition of walking, the response tasks, and the nature of the environments used.

Walking as an activity in the environment has been defined in a variety of ways: as walked versus not-walked paths (Cohen and Weatherford, 1980, 1981); as walk-plus-look versus look-only (Cohen, Weatherford, and Byrd, 1980; Herman and Siegel, 1978); and as self- versus other-directed movement (Feldman and Acredolo, 1979; Herman, 1980). Children have walked directly between locations (Cohen and Weatherford, 1980, 1981; Cohen, Weatherford, and Byrd, 1980); walked along a depicted "road" (Herman, 1980; Herman and Siegel, 1978); and walked along hallways in a building (Feldman and Acredolo, 1979).

As well as evaluating the nature of walking in different ways, researchers have assessed spatial representations in a variety of ways: distance estimates (Cohen and Weatherford, 1980; Cohen, Weatherford, and Byrd, 1980; reconstruction of the environment (Cohen and Weatherford, 1981; Herman, 1980; Herman and Siegel, 1978); and memory for the spatial location of an event (Feldman and Acredolo, 1979). These different tasks not only make different activity demands on the child (important as noted by Cohen, Weatherford, and Byrd, 1980) and different scaling demands (important as noted by Cohen and others, 1979; and Siegel and others, 1979), but they also make other logical demands, such as reorientation of judgments (see Cohen and others, 1979). The chapter by Lynn Liben in this volume discusses at greater length the important issue of response demands in relation to the externalization of spatial representations. The third source of variance among studies examining the role of activity—that is, the nature of the environment used—will be considered more fully here.

The environments used across these studies have been quite different: from common objects in a room setting (Cohen and Weatherford, 1980, 1981; Cohen, Weatherford, and Byrd, 1980), to a mock town (Herman, 1980; Herman and Siegel, 1978), to halls in a building (Feldman and Acredolo, 1979). All of these spaces were large in size and allowed for movement within them. However, some of these environments, albeit large in size, were nevertheless small in scale. That is, the entire space could be viewed from a single vantage point. Upon inspection, those studies showing a negligible effect of walking were in fact studies using large-in-size but small-in-scale environments. Those studies using large-scale environments showed positive benefits attributable to walking. David Weatherford's chapter in this volume analyzes the issue of small- versus large-scale spatial cognition. His dissertation research (Weatherford and Cohen, 1981), presented in that chapter, will be briefly reviewed here.

Third- and sixth-graders either walked a prescribed path through an experimental environment or received four successive views from the midpoint of each side. Screens prevented the children from viewing the environment while walking between designated viewing positions. In addition, the children experienced one of two environments; both environments contained an identical arrangement of six objects, but one contained barriers while the other did not. This manipulation allowed for an analysis of the activity conditions in relation to small- versus large-scale environments.

On the distance-estimation task that followed (again in an empty test room following acquisition), sixth-graders performed equally well in either activity condition for either type of environment. Third-graders equalled the performance of the older children for the barrier-free environment (that is, small-scale), for either activity condition. Differences in performance due to activity occurred for the large-scale environment. Third-graders who walked through the large-scale space estimated interlocation distances more accurately than those who only viewed the space from the perimeter.

The issue, then, is not whether walking is important for the construction of spatial representations but, rather, to whom and under what circumstances. Young children are aided by the sensorimotor information derived from walking when they are interacting with a truly large-scale environment, one that requires the coordination and integration of multiple percepts. Older children and adults seem able to use a variety of less physically active (but probably more cognitively active) means for achieving this integration.

In summary, the role of walking for the construction of spatial representations is complex. Environmental features such as barriers that obstruct movement and vision (indeed, create the large-scale nature of the space), the cognitive and developmental status of the participant within the space, and the tasks used to externalize the covert representation (in terms of both physical and logical demands) all interact to influence the participant's performance and our interpretations about the nature and functions of spatial representations.

Before deriving some general implications from our research, I would like to mention one additional project we have recently completed (Cohen and Cohen, forthcoming). In the vast majority of the experimental research on the influence of activity in spatial cognition, activity has been defined as movement between locations. However, people also perform activities *at* locations, and often it is the case that the activity at a location is dependent upon the completion of an activity at another location. This project examined the broader conceptualization of activity.

First- and sixth-graders served in three activity conditions. In the interact-linked condition, the child was told to write and mail a letter. The child picked up a pencil at location 1, walked to location 2, walked to location 3 and signed a piece of paper, walked to location 4, put the paper in an envelope and a stamp on the envelope, walked to location 5 and mailed the letter in a box, and returned the pencil to location 1. Thus the child performed activities at four of the five locations; some of the locations were functionally linked by activity while others were not.

The children in the second activity group, the interact-only group, also performed activities with the same materials as the interact-linked group at four of the five locations. However, these activities were designed so that no linking between activities (and thus between locations) occurred. Finally, those in the third activity condition, the walk-only group, merely walked the prescribed path, a condition similar to the walking condition in other studies.

Children gave all pairwise interlocation distance estimates in an empty test room following three acquisition trials. Sixth-graders were more accurate than first-graders overall. Children in the interact-linked group were more accurate than children in the other two activity groups that did not differ from each other. Thus, just performing activities at locations offered no advantage over simply walking. Interestingly, the benefit of functionally linking activity operated on both functionally linked and not functionally linked paths, whether walked or merely viewed. Providing a theme that interrelates environmental locations, then, appears to have a general facilitative effect for coordinating and integrating the entire environmental configuration.

Implications and New Directions

In concluding, four implications of our research into the role of activity for the construction of large-scale spatial cognition will be presented.

One of the hallmarks of research in the areas of both small- and large-scale spatial cognition is the prevalence of sex differences in performance (see Harris, 1981). Males often outperform females on tasks requiring these abilities. In our research we have witnessed main effects attributable to the sex of the subject (Cohen and Weatherford, 1981; Cohen, Weatherford, and Byrd, 1980). Interestingly, we have not gotten significant interactions between the sex of the subject and the various activity manipulations we have used. The ability of females to discriminate, analyze, and use spatial information may be different from that of males, yet females were influenced by activity experiences in the same manner as males.

The research reported here merely scratches the surface of the important issue of the externalization of internal representations. Liben (1981; see also her chapter in this volume) and Siegel, Kirasic, and Kail (1978) address this issue at greater length. When a child performs a spatial task, we assume some relationship between that performance and the internal representation that generates that performance. Obviously, our interpretations about representations rely heavily on that relationship. A growing body of literature indicates the tenuous nature of this link between task performance and internal representation. Both the logical demands of the task and the physical demands placed on responding influence performance and thus influence (perhaps in a misleading way) our interpretations of data.

Closely related to this issue of interpretation of data is the issue of the nature of the data collected in relation to the interpretations drawn. Researchers too often make inferences about an ability that is derived from the data but in fact may not be an ability directly "tapped" by the task. For example, some research reports under- and overestimations of responding from nondistance estimation response tasks. The experimenter derives distances on the basis of reconstructing the array or rank orderings, for example. Surely we are on shaky ground in making these ability inferences from derivations of the response measures. In sum, researchers (and consumers of research) must assess inferences about representations from tasks critically, as well as inferences about abilities derived but not directly assessed.

A third area affected by our research is scale of environment, which traditionally has been treated as a bipolar discontinuous dimension. The research reported here (Weatherford and Cohen, 1981) highlights the importance of a distinction of environments based on the necessity of multiple views. Perhaps, however, this dimension would be more fruitfully conceptualized as a continuum. For example, a room can require less integration and coordination of views than a city but more than a small model. The focus of research, then, becomes not one of trying to label the scale of the space but one of analyzing the type and degree of cognitive activity necessary to build a full representation of the space.

Finally, returning to the central theme of this chapter, there is a need for a more comprehensive definition and investigation of the role of activity. Our research and the work of others suggest that walking through an environment is an important activity, particularly for young children, particularly for spaces requiring multiple views. Upon reflection, however, movement in and of itself is not an important activity. Movement is the mode for bringing the individual into contact with the multiple views of a space. A molecular analysis of the cognitive activities that are served by movement (for example, attention, perception, and so forth) is needed. On the other hand, a more molar analysis beyond just walking is also necessary. The study on children's writing and mailing a letter (Cohen and Cohen, forthcoming) is a step in this direction. People walk to serve some other goals and activities. An investigation of these more global functional activities would be an important new direction toward a more comprehensive (and more ecologically valid) understanding of the role of activity for the construction of spatial representation.

References

Cohen, R., Baldwin, L. M., and Sherman, R. C. "Cognitive Maps of a Naturalistic Setting." *Child Development,* 1978, *49,* 1216–1218.

Cohen, R., and Weatherford, D. L. "Effects of Route Traveled on the Distance Estimates of Children and Adults." *Journal of Experimental Child Psychology,* 1980, *29,* 403–412.

Cohen, R., and Weatherford, D. L. "The Effect of Barriers on Spatial Representations." *Child Development,* 1981, *52,* 1087–1090.

Cohen, R., Weatherford, D. L., and Byrd, D. "Distance Estimates of Children as a Function of Acquisition and Response Activities." *Journal of Experimental Child Psychology,* 1980, *30,* 464–472.

Cohen, R., Weatherford, D. L., Lomenick, T., and Koeller, K. "Development of Spatial Representations: Role of Task Demands and Familiarity with the Environment." *Child Development,* 1979, *50,* 1257–1260.

Cohen, S., and Cohen, R. "Distance Estimates of Children as a Function of Type of Activity in the Environment." *Child Development,* forthcoming.

Feldman, A. L., and Acredolo, L. P. "The Effect of Active Versus Passive Exploration on Memory for Spatial Locations." *Child Development,* 1979, *50,* 698–704.

Harris, L. J. "Sex-Related Variations in Spatial Skill." In L. S. Liben, A. H. Patterson, and N. Newcombe (Eds.), *Spatial Representation and Behavior Across the Life Span.* New York: Academic Press, 1981.

Herman, J. F. "Children's Cognitive Maps of Large-Scale Spaces: Effects of Exploration, Direction, and Repeated Experience." *Journal of Experimental Child Psychology,* 1980, *29,* 126–143.

Herman, J. F., and Siegel, A. W. "The Development of Cognitive Mapping of the Large-Scale Environment." *Journal of Experimental Child Psychology,* 1978, *26,* 389–406.

50

Ittelson, W. H. "Environment Perception and Contemporary Perceptual Theory." In W. H. Ittelson (Ed.), *Environment and Cognition.* New York: Seminar Press, 1973.

Kosslyn, S. M., Pick, H., and Fariello, G. R. "Cognitive Maps in Children and Men." *Child Development,* 1974, *45,* 707–716.

Lee, T. R. "Perceived Distance as a Function of Direction in the City." *Environment and Behavior,* 1970, *2,* 40–51.

Liben, L. S. "Spatial Representation and Behavior: Multiple Perspectives." In L. S. Liben, A. H. Patterson, and N. Newcombe (Eds.), *Spatial Representation and Behavior Across the Life Span.* New York: Academic Press, 1981.

Liben, L. S., Patterson, A. H., and Newcombe, N. (Eds.). *Spatial Representation and Behavior Across the Life Span.* New York: Academic Press, 1981.

Siegel, A. W., Herman, J. F., Allen, G. L., and Kirasic, K. C. "The Development of Cognitive Maps of Large- and Small-Scale Spaces." *Child Development,* 1979, *50,* 582–585.

Siegel, A. W., Kirasic, K. C., and Kail, R. V. "Stalking the Elusive Cognitive Map." In J. F. Wohlwill and I. Altman (Eds.), *Human Behavior and the Environment.* New York: Plenum, 1978.

Siegel, A. W., and White, S. H. "The Development of Spatial Representations of Large-Scale Environments." In H. W. Reese (Ed.), *Advances in Child Development and Behavior.* Vol. 10. New York: Academic Press, 1975.

Weatherford, D. L., and Cohen, R. "The Influence of Locomotor Activity on Spatial Representation." Paper presented at the biennial meeting of the Society for Research in Child Development, Boston, April 3, 1981.

Robert Cohen is an assistant professor of psychology at Memphis State University. In addition to working in the research program on the development of spatial cognition, he is also involved in research examining clinical and educational interventions in the context of developmental change.

Children's difficulties in drawing accurate sketch maps led earlier researchers to conclude that young children were spatially incompetent. More recently, investigators have devised new large-scale spatial tasks on which children perform well. How do our tasks affect our conclusions about children's spatial cognition?

Children's Large-Scale Spatial Cognition: Is the Measure the Message?

Lynn S. Liben

Introduction: Issues in Assessing Spatial Cognition

Much of the current research in children's spatial cognition has its roots in the work described by Piaget and Inhelder (1956) in *The Child's Conception of Space.* Piaget and Inhelder were interested in demonstrating that spatial concepts—like other concepts such as time, number, and causality—are constructed by the child through interactions with the environment and change qualitatively with development.

Piaget and Inhelder proposed that children first master topological concepts of space that concern relations of neighborhood, continuity, separation, and order. Because topological spatial relations are concerned only with ele-

Support for the preparation of this chapter, and for portions of the research described in it, was provided in part by BRSG Grant S07 RR07084–14 awarded to the University of Pittsburgh by the Biomedical Research Support Grant Program, Division of Research Resources, National Institutes of Health. The insightful comments of Roger Downs, Nora Newcombe, and Lynne Curtis on an earlier version of this manuscript are gratefully acknowledged.

R. Cohen (Ed.). *New Directions for Child Development: Children's Conceptions of Spatial Relationships,* no. 15. San Francisco: Jossey-Bass, March 1982.

51

ments of a single object or configuration, they permit neither the location of objects within a global space, nor the appreciation of changing points of view, nor the measurement of metric distances. In contrast, these operations are possible with the construction of projective spatial concepts (which concern the coordination of various perspectives) and the construction of Euclidean spatial concepts (which establish a reference system that is totally independent of a particular point of view). Piaget and Inhelder (1956) argued that projective and Euclidean concepts are acquired in middle and late childhood. (See Laurendeau and Pinard, 1970, for a more complete discussion of topological, projective, and Euclidean concepts and their development; see Liben, 1981, for a more general discussion of concepts of space).

The most relevant of the Piagetian paradigms for the topic of this volume — large-scale spatial cognition — is research on children's ability to produce representations of their familiar environments. In one study, for example, children were given a sand tray with wet sand and materials to represent buildings, greens, parks, bridges, and rivers. After putting one building in the middle of the sand tray, the experimenter told the child "Now this is the big school. . . . There are plenty more houses, little ones and big ones. These little bits of wood are to make bridges with and this blue ribbon is the Arve. Now I want to know everything near the school. You put things in the right places" (Piaget, Inhelder, and Szeminska, 1960, p. 5). Children were also asked to draw maps in the sand or on paper to show how they go from home to school or to another well-known landmark. After completing these tasks, the experimenter rotated the model school building 180 degrees and asked "Now if I turn the school around like this, must we move everything else about as well or can we leave it just as it is?"

Piaget and Inhelder (1956) and Piaget, Inhelder, and Szeminska (1960) report that the responses of children in stages I or II, typically below the age of seven, are egocentric, uncoordinated, and irreversible. More specifically, their reactions may be characterized in three ways. First, their descriptions of routes are tied directly to their own actions, "as though these were some kind of absolute, and the various landmarks are fixed in terms of them instead of vice versa" (Piaget, Inhelder, and Szeminska, 1960, p. 6). Second, the landmarks are not organized in terms of an objective spatial whole. Thus, pairs of landmarks are unrelated to other landmarks in the system, with subjective considerations (for example, affective value) directing the placement of various points. Third, these children are unable to rotate a map or model and unable to reconstruct a route in a reverse direction.

At the next stage, IIIA, children show limited coordinations so that, within clusters of landmarks, relationships are correct, but across these clusters relationships are haphazard. Finally, in stage IIIB, children are able to integrate both within and between clusters, to represent the routes in forward and backward directions, and to rearrange the rotated plan correctly.

On the basis of these and similar studies, most developmental psychologists concluded that young children do not have well-developed spatial concepts. More recently, however, perhaps as part of the growing Zeitgeist that emphasizes young children's cognitive competencies rather than their incompetencies (see, for example, Flavell, 1977; Siegler, 1978), investigators have begun to use other tasks to assess children's spatial cognition. The basic argument is that young children may actually have very good representations of their spatial world but are unable to demonstrate these representations because they cannot meet the extraneous demands of the traditional Piagetian tasks. For example, in discussing the use of sketch maps, verbal descriptions, and construction of small-scale models, Siegel (1981) suggests that "these techniques tend to lead to underestimates of children's spatial competence because they confound spatial knowledge with externalizing ability and other theoretically nonrelevant task loads" (p. 190).

In keeping with this argument, there has been a growing trend to deemphasize tasks such as those originally designed by Piaget and Inhelder (1956) and to replace them with new empirical methods. One approach has been to infer children's spatial representations from their ability to move through space in direct locomotion tasks. For example, children's success in wayfinding (as in getting from home to school) has been cited as evidence for the existence of children's spatial representations. A second approach has been to derive coordinated spatial representations from performance on tasks that do not themselves require the direct production of an integrated spatial representation. The latter approach is illustrated, for example, by tasks in which children are asked to make rank judgments about the relative distances of objects. Multidimensional scaling techniques are then applied to the children's rank ordered judgments, and the derived map is taken as a model of the child's underlying spatial representation.

The major thesis presented in this chapter is that great caution should be exercised before drawing inferences about children's underlying spatial representations from either of these two approaches. First, it is argued that not all locomotive behaviors "tap" spatial representation, even when different interpretations of the term *spatial representation* are taken into account. Second, it is asserted that, when a series of individual judgments on a spatial task is used to derive an integrated spatial representation, the inferred representation does not necessarily reflect the subject's internalized representation. Indeed, it is argued even more generally that the pattern of responses from any single task cannot provide conclusive information about the subject's spatial representation. Rather, multiple assessments are required because performance on any given task is affected not only by the child's spatial representation but also by the child's manipulation of that information and, further, by the experimenter's manipulation of the child's manipulation (that is, the way in which the raw data are analyzed).

Siegel (1981) also emphasizes the importance of task demands. He asserts that children's sketch maps and models are determined by children's spatial representational skills as well as their ability to meet nonspatial task demands. The emphasis here, however, is different. Siegel concludes that to obtain a "true" picture of children's spatial representations, it is necessary to avoid mapping, modeling, and so forth. The point made here is that performance on *any* task always includes cognitive manipulation, and, thus, one can never determine the "true" representation from a single task (see also Downs, 1981; Liben, 1981; Newcombe, 1981; Newcombe and Liben, forthcoming). The remainder of this chapter is devoted to discussing these points in more detail and to illustrating them by reference to current empirical research.

Locomotion and Spatial Representation

The relationship between behaviors in space and representation of space is a complex one. In one sense, spatial activities are necessarily involved in all measures of spatial representation, insofar as subjects must do something active (be it moving a pencil, pointing to a picture, or walking along a route) to respond to a spatial task. As soon as one goes beyond this necessary but trivial relationship, however, the link between spatial behavior and spatial representation becomes more controversial.

One theoretical position is that the ability to act in space does not reflect the ability to represent space. In taking this position, Piaget (1970; Piaget and Inhelder, 1956) distinguishes specifically between *practical space,* which is the capacity to act in space, and *conceptual space,* which is the capacity to represent space. Piaget argues that the ability to act in space no more implies the ability to represent space than "the fact that the child breathes, digests, and possesses a heart that beats [implies] that he has any idea of alimentary metabolism or the circulatory system" (Piaget and Inhelder, 1956, p. 378).

The alternative position is that the child's ability to locomote through space is indeed indicative of underlying spatial representation. Acredolo, Pick, and Olsen (1975), for example, argue that "as long as the large-scale spatial task one chooses in some way requires the children to draw from past experience with the spatial layout of an environment, one is still assessing representational abilities even though they are not being manifested in the external representations typical of the developmental literature to date" (p. 495). In one implementation of this approach, Acredolo, Pick, and Olsen (1975) took preschoolers on a walk through various kinds of environments and later asked them to return to particular locations (for example, the place where some keys had been dropped). Chldren's ability to return to the point accurately was taken as a measure of spatial representation.

Locomotion behaviors outside the laboratory have also been pointed to as indicators of spatial representation. Siegel, Kirasic, and Kail (1978), for example, suggest that children's wayfinding is based upon underlying representations, thereby arguing that the developmental increments in wayfinding ability are "attributable, in large part, to developmental changes in cognitive mapping skills. . . . That is, we assume that accurate wayfinding in the large environment is guided by some reasonably accurate internal representation of that environment—a cognitive map [Downs and Stea, 1973]—and that the characteristics of these internal representations change developmentally [Stea and Blaut, 1973]" (p. 224).

Whether or not the ability to negotiate through space is taken as an indication of spatial representation depends in part on what is actually meant by the term *spatial representation*. As discussed elsewhere (Liben, 1981), the term spatial representation has been used in three major ways. First, it can refer to the observable, external *spatial products* such as sketch maps, verbal descriptions, or scale models, that are used to represent space. The second and third meanings refer to internal spatial representations, which are of more relevance here. *Spatial thought* refers to conscious knowledge about space— that is, spatial knowledge that individuals reflect upon or manipulate, as in mental rotation tasks or in imagining spatial layouts of living rooms. *Spatial storage* is knowledge about space that is stored in some form but to which the individual (or investigator) has no immediate access. We can only infer that certain information about the space must be stored to enable the individual to have acted in a particular manner. However, the particular form of that knowledge is inaccessible, and can be modeled by the investigator in any one of a number of ways (for example, by cartographic maps, lists of coordinate point locations).

Successful performance on either of the two locomotion tasks described above implies internal spatial representation, at least in the sense of spatial storage: Some information about locations must be stored in some form to permit the individual to return to a particular place or to go from home to school. One might, however, perform these locomotion tasks without conscious spatial representations of the space, and, thus, the behaviors need not reveal the content of spatial thought. For example, in going from home to school, the child might have stored a series of isolated kinesthetic-perceptual pieces of information, so that, for example, when the traffic light comes into view, he or she automatically turns to the right and walks one block. That is, the child need not necessarily base finding his or her way on a cognitive map, if we interpret cognitive map as a cartographic, map-like representation, albeit one that is "stripped down . . . distorted, fragmented, and often inaccurate" (Siegel, Kirasic, and Kail, 1978, p. 225). Similarly, an adult might get to his or her bed in a darkened room without bumping into the dresser, even without an integrated, map-like representation of the bedroom. Kinesthetic memories (based on prior bruises) might serve to direct movements.

While locomotor behaviors of these kinds would presumably not be pertinent to the kinds of spatial concepts of interest to Piaget (for whom relevant tasks are those, like mapping, that require spatial thought), these behaviors are informative to investigators interested in other aspects of spatial cognition (see Liben, 1981). In short, the identical locomotor behaviors may be taken as indicators of spatial representations by some investigators but not by others because of different interpretations of the concept of spatial representation.

Importantly, however, some locomotion tasks do not require (and thus, fail to reveal) internal spatial representation in either interpretation of the term. Instead, these locomotion tasks can be solved on the basis of perceptual feedback. In these cases, it is critical to avoid inferring underlying representations (consciously accessible or not) on the basis of locomotion.

This point may be illustrated by reference to work initiated by Siegel and Schadler (1977), who argue that the graphic and verbal demands of tasks such as those used by Piaget and Inhelder mask young children's knowledge of familiar spatial environments. To eliminate verbal and graphic demands, Siegel and Schadler asked kindergarteners to construct, from memory, a tabletop model of their everyday classroom using furniture that had been made to scale. Although some children produced extremely accurate reconstructions, others were grossly inaccurate. One now famous kindergartener — Buffy — simply clustered all the furniture in the center of the model room.

Siegel (1981) notes, however, despite this inaccurate model, Buffy was never "seen bumping into walls in [her] classroom" and suggests then that the "source of Buffy's poor performance is not in her internal representation of the classroom but rather in the technique used to externalize the children's spatial knowledge (that is, their cognitive maps)" (p. 172). It is possible, however, that Buffy is able to avoid bumping into walls simply by reference to the visual information immediately available to her, rather than by reference to an "internal representation" of her classroom. The issue here, then, is whether Buffy's navigational competence does, in fact, reflect underlying representation.

In response to this issue, a recent study (Liben, Moore, and Golbeck, forthcoming) was conducted to determine if children would reveal spatial knowledge of their classroom environments with a task that allows normal motoric and sensory feedback (for example, walking between objects, seeing the relationships among objects). An inability to perform well on a task of this kind would reflect incomplete spatial representations (even in the sense of spatial storage).

Twenty preschool children ranging in age from 3½ to 5½ years (mean age, 4½) were given several tasks that concerned their highly familiar preschool classroom. These tasks were also given to ten college women who had been student teachers in the same classroom.

In one task, subjects were asked to produce a scale model of their classroom. More specifically, subjects were shown a model room (one inch = one foot) that included detailed colored drawings representing the windows, decorations, exits, and so forth, as well as several pieces of permanent furniture. Model furniture was made to scale from balsa wood, decorated to correspond to the real furniture (for example, miniature art materials, books, and so forth were attached to the models). Subjects were asked to place twenty-five pieces of furniture into the model classroom to show their usual locations. This modeling task, then, was like that used by Siegel and Schadler (1977).

The second task was identical to the first, except that, rather than asking subjects to reproduce the arrangement of their classroom with a scale model, we asked the subjects to arrange the furniture in their actual classroom. To do so, all but several pieces of heavy furniture (these constituted the permanent furniture in the model task) were removed from the room, and the subject was asked (with the physical assistance of the experimenter) to put each piece of furniture "exactly where it is when you come to school in the morning."

In both the model and classroom settings, the complete layout task provides rich relational cues that may either facilitate or depress children's ability to locate pieces of furniture. For example, the child may not know the position of the toy stove in the abstract (that is, its coordinates with respect to axes defined by classroom walls) but may know that the toy stove is next to the toy sink. If, then, the child first places the toy sink in the correct location, the child would place the stove correctly. Alternatively, if the toy sink is placed incorrectly, the toy stove will be misplaced as well.

We were, therefore, interested in testing subjects' knowledge of furniture locations in a way that could not draw on the vast number of topological and relational cues that are normally present in reconstruction tasks. The most extreme elimination of cues would occur in a blindfolding task. A blindfolding task, however, also removes from view the stable referent axes (classroom walls). In addition, results of pilot work showed that even an adult who was highly familiar with the preschool classroom (a supervising teacher) found the task of walking between familiar classroom landmarks while blindfolded an extremely anxiety-provoking task. Thus, the task we used in our research was one that allowed subjects to see all frame cues but eliminated relational cues (correct or incorrect) that would normally have resulted from prior furniture placements. More specifically, subjects were asked to locate pieces of furniture one at a time. By removing each item after it had been placed, relational cues from one placement were not visible to prejudice the placement of subsequent items.

For pragmatic reasons, only six items of furniture were used in this isolated location task. The six items were selected so that half were *bounded*—that is, bordered on permanent, topological cues (for example, the toy refrigerator, which was located next to the heating unit) and half were *unbounded*—that is, did not adjoin permanent features (for example, the toy sink, which was located away from all other permanent furniture and walls.) Because we wanted to avoid having the actual pieces of furniture moved for this task, we asked subjects to place cardboard forms in the size and shape of the bottom of the piece of furniture model. Subjects placed the forms one at a time, with the experimenter removing each form after recording its position. Performance on both tasks was scored with respect to the number of items placed at the correct location (within 1½ feet in the classroom, within 1½ inches in the model).

Adults performed virtually perfectly on all tasks, and, thus, their data were omitted from statistical analyses. Children, however, performed with considerably more variability. As expected, performance in the classroom setting was significantly better than performance with the model for the complete layout task (with a maximum of 25 correct placements, means were 14.4 versus 6.8 correct in the two settings, respectively). This relationship was also evident on the isolated location task (with a maximum score of 6 correct, combining bounded and unbounded items, mean scores were 2.6 versus 1.7 for classroom and model settings, respectively). Also as expected, performance on the bounded items of the location task was significantly higher than performance on the unbounded items (with a maximum score of 3, means were 1.3 versus .9). It is noteworthy that the absolute errors in the inaccurate placements were not trivial: The average placement error was approximately 8 feet!

Two major conclusions from the findings of this study are of relevance here. First, it does appear that, as Siegel (1981) argues, young children do have more knowledge about the spatial arrangements of their classrooms than they demonstrate in tabletop modeling tasks. Children are more successful in locating individual pieces of furniture (the location task) and in duplicating the full room arrangement (the complete layout task) when asked to do so in their actual classroom than when asked to do so in a small-scale model.

The second conclusion, however, is that, while performance is better in the classroom, it is far from universally good. Some children are still woefully inaccurate even in placing their actual furniture back in their actual classroom. In view of the extensive kinesthetic and sensory feedback available in the classroom, the inability to perform well on this task suggests that some children do not, in fact, have good spatial representations of their classrooms (even in the sense of spatial storage). Although there is always some possibility that these children's difficulties stem from an inability to understand task instructions, anecdotal data did not provide support for this interpretation. Thus, it appears that some children's difficulties on standard spatial tasks lie much deeper than an inability to meet the demands of "the technique used to externalize the children's spatial knowledge" (Siegel, 1981, p. 172). For some children, success in navigating through the classroom environment without bumping into walls is apparently based on the ability to process perceptual information, rather than the ability to draw upon internal spatial representation.

Derived Spatial Representations

As already noted, most early studies of environmental knowledge required subjects to produce sketch maps or models of their environments.

Two problems with this technique have been noted. One is that psychologists typically evaluate the accuracy of subjects' sketch maps against a particular cartographic map without recognizing that the cartographic map is *itself* only a metaphor for reality (see Downs, 1981, for an extensive discussion of this issue). Second, and of more relevance here, the production of sketch maps (or scale models) has been criticized for taxing subjects' graphic and scale-reduction skills, thought to be particularly problematic for children.

In response to the latter criticism, investigators have developed new tasks in which subjects are asked to make a series of individual judgments which are then integrated mathematically to produce a model of the subject's spatial representation. An important contrast between older procedures (sketch maps, models) and new procedures (for example, rank ordering of relative distances, see Kosslyn, Pick, and Fariello, 1974; triangulation, see Hardwick, McIntyre, and Pick, 1976; projective convergence, see Curtis, Siegel, and Furlong, 1981) is that, whereas the former provide direct information about subjects' representation of interrelationships among locations, the latter infer those relationships mathematically. For example, a sketch map provides direct information about topological relationships among items (for example, the church is next to the school) and information about metric distance (the church is twice as far from the library as it is from the bus station). Derived representations, in contrast, take subjects' individual judgments (such as distance and direction information from a series of sighting locations) and integrate them into a unified representation through devices such as multidimensional scaling (MDS). The argument here is that it is important not to overinterpret the qualities of the derived representations. That is, one cannot claim that the derived representation is fully isomorphic with the subject's actual representation (spatial thought).

Several lines of evidence support the need for caution. The first is logical. Different mathematical procedures yield different derived representations. For example, in multidimensional scaling, data can be fit equally well with solutions specifying different numbers of dimensions. Obviously, if different derived maps are possible, no one map can be taken as necessarily veridical.

A second line of evidence is derived from research concerning subjects' own evaluations of direct versus derived maps. Specifically, Baird, Merrill, and Tannenbaum (1979) asked adult subjects to perform two kinds of spatial tasks concerning their highly familiar (campus or town) environment. In one task, subjects were asked to create maps of the environment directly, by showing the location of eleven buildings. In the other task, subjects were asked for numerical estimates of relative distances between all pairs of the eleven buildings, which were then subjected to MDS to produce a two-dimensional map. More variability among subjects was found on the latter task. Furthermore, subjects judged their direct maps to be more accurate than the derived maps, an evaluation that concurred with judgments of a new group of subjects who had not been involved in producing the direct maps in the first place.

A third line of evidence comes from the results of a series of studies that Nora Newcombe and I have been conducting, in which a variety of dependent measures are used to examine the appearance of barrier effects. This program of research builds upon a paradigm originated by Kosslyn, Pick, and Fariello (1974). These investigators first had kindergarten children and adults learn the location of ten toys in a seventeen-foot square space divided into quadrants by transparent barriers in one direction and opaque barriers in the other. The toy locations were distributed in such a way that some pairs of objects were separated by three feet and others by five feet. In addition, pairs were separated by no barrier, by a transparent barrier, or by an opaque barrier.

After learning the locations of all ten toys, subjects were asked to rank order toys with respect to how close they were to a referent toy. Thus, subjects were given a toy as a referent and asked which of the remaining nine toys was closest to the referent toy, which was next closest, next closest, and so on, until all nine toys had been named. Each toy served once as referent.

From these rank ordering judgments, the number of intervening items named between critical pairs was calculated. The particularly interesting developmental finding reported by Kosslyn, Pick, and Fariello (1974) was an age by barrier interaction. For children, either kind of barrier led to an exaggeration of the distance between pairs (as measured by the number of intervening items named on the rank ordering judgments). For adults, only the opaque barrier led to an exaggeration of the number of intervening items.

Two possible explanations for the more pervasive barrier effects in children are possible. One is that children exaggerate distances between objects when direct travel between objects is prohibited, as is the case for either type of barrier. Another possibility is that children need to organize the space into smaller subspaces than do adults because of their quantitatively more limited information-processing capacities. Hence, children use both kinds of barriers to organize the space into quadrants, whereas adults use only the more salient of the two kinds of barriers to organize the space into halves.

In either of these two cases, it is possible that the representation itself reflects the distortion, so that, for example, pairs that are actually separated by five feet with an intervening barrier would be represented by the subject (in spatial thought and/or storage) as further apart from one another than are objects separated by five feet without intervening barriers. Alternatively, barrier and no-barrier pairs might be represented equivalently, with the cognitive manipulations of the represented information yielding observed barrier effects. In the former case, one should find evidence for barrier effects across dependent measures. In the latter case, the observation of barrier effects should be susceptible to changes in task demands.

To explore these issues, Nora Newcombe and I (Newcombe and Liben, forthcoming) tested one group of subjects (first graders and college students) by asking for rank ordering (as in Kosslyn, Pick, and Fariello, 1974) and a second group of subjects by asking for direct estimates of the distances between pairs of items. These two tasks are of interest because their processing demands differ. To make the comparative judgments needed for rank ordering task, subjects must consider the entire space simultaneously. To estimate distances between pairs, subjects need consider only two objects at a time. If children's difficulty on rank ordering tasks stems from a difficulty in keeping the entire space in mind simultaneously because of a limited processing capacity, then barrier effects should be present for the rank ordering measure only. If, however, young children's difficulty stems from equating actual distance with functional distance, then barrier effects should be evident for both the rank ordering measure and the distance estimate measure.

Strikingly, the pattern of results was found to differ for the two measures. With the rank ordering measure, there was a significant age by barrier interaction, thus replicating the results of Kosslyn, Pick, and Fariello (1974). With the direct distance estimates, however, this interaction was absent. These findings are consistent with the hypothesis that developmental differences appear in relation to the cognitive manipulations required by a particular task (spatial thought), rather than necessarily residing in the information that subjects have about the space itself (spatial storage).

We are now trying to clarify the conditions under which barrier effects occur with the rank ordering measure. For example, we have asked adults to make rank ordering judgments when the space contains twenty rather than ten toys, to see if an increase in demand on processing capacity (cognitive overload) might cause adults to behave like children (that is, to show barrier effects for both kinds of barriers). Findings show that, adults do, indeed, show a pattern like children—that is, exaggerating distances across transparent as well as opaque barriers (Liben and Newcombe, 1981). In another study with children, we substituted two different patterns of masking tape for the physical barriers. Of interest was whether children would exaggerate distances across these pseudo barriers, which do not prevent locomotion but can be used for subdividing the space. Again, at the longer (five-foot) distance, barrier effects were found for both kinds of tapes.

In both of these studies, we also asked subjects to produce maps of the space by placing small pictures of the objects on paper to show their location. Distances between pairs separated by barriers were not exaggerated relative to pairs not separated by barriers, even for the longer distances. Thus, the barrier effects found with the rank ordering measure in the adult (overload) study or in the children (tape) study were not paralleled in subjects' maps.

While it is obvious that much more research is needed to determine the factors influencing barrier effects, the existing data are adequate to demonstrate that the emergence of barrier effects is susceptible to the dependent measure employed: Different patterns of barrier effects were found with rank ordering judgments, direct distance estimates, and map constructions. As discussed earlier, this inconsistency across measures suggests that points separated by barriers are probably not exaggerated in spatial storage. More generally, it demonstrates the impropriety of drawing conclusions about internal representations on the basis of findings from any single dependent measure.

Thus, while it may, indeed, be true that young children have more difficulty than adults in externalizing what they know about space in tasks such as those devised by Piaget and Inhelder (1956), it is not legitimate simply to substitute maps derived from other dependent measures and assume that these externalize the underlying representation more accurately.

Summary and Conclusions

The study of children's large-scale spatial cognition has passed through at least two major phases during the last few decades. In the 1950s and 1960s, investigators used tasks that required direct productions of subjects' spatial representations. Findings from these tasks led investigators to conclude that spatial cognition of young children was qualitatively and quantitatively worse than that of older children and adults. More recently, investigators have attempted to find age appropriate indicators of children's large-scale spatial cognition. The thesis of this chapter has been that these new approaches must be treated with great caution.

First, it was argued that children's ability to move successfully through an environment cannot in itself be taken as evidence that the child has an internal representation of that environment. This is not to assert that locomotor behaviors can never tap representations but rather that they do not necessarily do so. Second, it was argued that even tasks that undeniably draw upon subjects' internal knowledge about space do not necessarily yield representations that are isomorphic with the stored information: Any task requires that the subject manipulate what he or she knows about a space. *A priori*, it is just as reasonable to attribute observed developmental differences to differences in the way that knowledge is manipulated (spatial thought) as to attribute them to differences in the knowledge itself (spatial storage).

The latter point raises a more general issue concerning the focus of research on spatial cognition. There seems to be an assumption in much work on large-scale spatial cognition that what we are ultimately interested in is the content of the "mind's eye." From this perspective, we should use any possible avenue of reducing the cognitive manipulations of what is known about the space. Alternatively, we might well define the manipulations themselves as the competence of interest. From this perspective, the appropriate research strategy is to vary the manipulation demands systematically and observe the outcomes on developmental patterns. A strategy of this kind, such as the competence-activation/utilization approach outlined by Overton and Newman (forthcoming) "provides a more integrated and realistic perspective than one that focuses on a single component and treats other features as noise or error" (manuscript p. 34; see also Downs, 1981).

In short, the developmental study of large-scale spatial cognition should be ready to pass into a third phase, in which the emphasis is no longer on which is the best means of externalizing children's spatial representations but is instead on trying to identify the cognitive strategies used to organize and extract spatial information and determining how these change with development.

References

Acredolo, L. P., Pick, H. L., and Olsen, M. G. "Environmental Differentiation and Familiarity as Determinants of Children's Memory for Spatial Location." *Developmental Psychology,* 1975, *11,* 495–501.

Baird, J. C., Merrill, A. A., and Tannenbaum, J. "Cognitive Representation of Spatial Relations: II. A Familiar Environment." *Journal of Experimental Psychology: General,* 1979, *108,* 92–98.

Curtis, L. E., Siegel, A. W., and Furlong, N. E. "Developmental Differences in Cognitive Mapping: Configurational Knowledge of Familiar Large-Scale Environments." *Journal of Experimental Child Psychology,* 1981, *31,* 456–469.

Downs, R. M. "Maps and Mapping as Metaphors for Spatial Representation." In L. S. Liben, A. H. Patterson, and N. Newcombe (Eds.), *Spatial Representation and Behavior Across the Life Span.* New York: Academic Press, 1981.

Downs, R. M., and Stea, D. (Eds.). *Image and Environment: Cognitive Mapping and Spatial Behavior.* Chicago: Aldine, 1973.

Flavell, J. *Cognitive Development.* Englewood Cliffs, N.J.: Prentice-Hall, 1977.

Hardwick, D. A., McIntyre, C. W., and Pick, H. L. "The Content and Manipulation of Cognitive Maps in Children and Adults." *Monographs of the Society for Research in Child Development,* 1976, *41* (entire issue).

Kosslyn, S. M., Pick, H. L., and Fariello, G. R. "Cognitive Maps in Children and Men." *Child Development,* 1974, *45,* 707–716.

Laurendeau, M., and Pinard, A. *The Development of the Concept of Space in the Child.* New York: International Universities Press, 1970.

Liben, L. S. "Spatial Representation and Behavior: Multiple Perspectives." In L. S. Liben, A. H. Patterson, and N. Newcombe (Eds.), *Spatial Representation and Behavior Across the Life Span.* New York: Academic Press, 1981.

Liben, L. S., Moore, M. L., and Golbeck, S. L. "Preschoolers' Knowledge of Their Classroom Environment: Evidence from Small-Scale and Life-Size Spatial Tasks." *Child Development,* forthcoming.

Liben, L. S., and Newcombe, N. "Barrier Effects and Processing Demands." Paper presented at the meetings of the Psychonomic Society, Philadelphia, November 1981.

Newcombe, N. "Spatial Representation and Behavior: Retrospect and Prospect." In L. S. Liben, A. H. Patterson, and N. Newcombe (Eds.), *Spatial Representation and Behavior Across the Life Span.* New York: Academic Press, 1981.

Newcombe, N., and Liben, L. "Barrier Effects in the Cognitive Maps of Children and Adults." *Journal of Experimental Child Psychology,* forthcoming.

Overton, W. F., and Newman, J. L. "Cognitive Development: A Competence-Activation/Utilization Approach." In T. Field, A. Huston, H. Quay, L. Troll, and G. Finley (Eds.), *Review of Human Development.* New York: Wiley, forthcoming.

Piaget, J. *Genetic Epistemology.* New York: Norton, 1970.

Piaget, J., and Inhelder, B. *The Child's Conception of Space.* New York: Norton, 1956.

Piaget, J., Inhelder, B., and Szeminska, A. *The Child's Conception of Geometry.* New York: Basic Books, 1960.

Siegel, A. W. "The Externalization of Cognitive Maps by Children and Adults: In Search of Ways to Ask Better Questions." In L. S. Liben, A. H. Patterson, and N. Newcombe (Eds.), *Spatial Representation and Behavior Across the Life Span.* New York: Academic Press, 1981.

Siegel, A. W., Kirasic, K. C., and Kail, R. V. "Stalking the Elusive Cognitive Map." In J. F. Wohlwill and I. Altman (Eds.), *Human Behavior and Environment.* Vol. 3. New York: Plenum, 1978.

Siegel, A. W., and Schadler, M. "Young Children's Cognitive Maps of Their Classroom." *Child Development,* 1977, *48,* 388–394.

Siegler, R. S. (Ed.). *Children's Thinking: What Develops?* Hillsdale, N.J.: Erlbaum, 1978.

Stea, D., and Blaut, J. M. "Toward a Developmental Theory of Spatial Learning." In R. M. Downs and D. Stea (Eds.), *Image and Environment: Cognitive Mapping and Spatial Behavior.* Chicago: Aldine, 1973.

Lynn S. Liben is associate professor of psychology and head of the
developmental psychology area at the University of Pittsburgh, where
she is also a Center Associate of the Learning Research and Development
Center. After receiving her doctorate from the University of Michigan,
she served on the faculties of the University of Rochester and the
Pennsylvania State University. Her research concerns the development
of memory, spatial concepts, and deaf children.

Study of the development of spatial cognition has become a semi-autonomous subfield in the study of cognitive development. But, as well as generating knowledge about the nature of spatial representation and behavior in children and adults, the study of spatial cognition raises fundamental, and perennial, questions about the nature of cognitive development and the methodology of cognitive-developmental research.

Development of Spatial Cognition and Cognitive Development

Nora Newcombe

As Gary Allen observes in Chapter Three (this volume), about a decade ago a surge of activity began in the study of spatial cognition. Papers published at that time frequently opened by stating that psychologists knew almost nothing about how people perceive and think about spatial layouts. There were some signposts: Tolman's (1948) work with rats was often cited as precedent for use of the term *cognitive map* and Piaget's work on children's concepts of space (Piaget and Inhelder, 1956) was referred to with respect. But there was consensus that we were in dire need of data to supplement theorizing about the nature of developmental change in knowledge of space.

In the past few years, we have gathered quite a lot of the needed data. Although many unanswered questions remain, great progress has been made in understanding how to study spatial thought (see, for example, comments by Liben and also by Cohen in this volume on choices of dependent variables) and in formulating some of the key conceptual distinctions which may be vital to allowing generalizations of conclusions across contexts (see Weatherford's chapter in this volume on the nature of the distinction between large- and small-scale space). In reaching for these achievements, however, the study of

I would like to thank Lynn Liben, William Dundon, Barbara Rogoff, and Mary Gauvain for commenting on this chapter.

R. Cohen (Ed.). *New Directions for Child Development: Children's Conceptions of Spatial Relationships*, no. 15. San Francisco: Jossey-Bass, March 1982.

spatial cognition has diverged from the mainstream of the study of cognitive development, and has become established as a separate subfield with its own concerns and methods of inquiry.

As Allen also observes in his chapter, now may be the time to consider what we have learned in the past decade. In particular, I would like to argue that the knowledge we have gained and the methodological problems we have encountered are not specific to the subfield. Rather, the experience of the past decade also bears upon issues of perennial interest in the study of cognitive development. In the first part of this chapter, I will consider methodology. Specifically, the effect of context on children's performance has recently emerged as a concern for many developmentalists; a second problem involves choices of dependent variables and questions arising when results differ depending on the variables used. Quandaries concerning these issues arise in the study of spatial cognition, as in other areas of inquiry. In the second part of the chapter, I will discuss how the study of spatial cognition relates to general questions about the existence of stages in cognitive development, the reasons for age-related cognitive change and the possible parallels between the thought of adults and of children. In this second section, I will consider three proposals concerning the nature of developmental change in spatial cognition, specifically, the hypotheses that children progress from use of topological to use of Euclidean frames of reference, progress from landmark to route to con-figurational knowledge of their environments, and acquire the capacity to conserve distance and length, which aids their ability to deal with large-scale spaces. For each of these three proposals, I will examine both the evidence concerning children's hypothesized lack of competence, and adults' supposed possession of it, arguing that we need to know more about the limits of both child and adult competence before we can talk with confidence about the existence and nature of these developmental progressions.

Cognitive Development and Spatial Development: Methodological Concerns

Context and Conclusions. A concern for the experimental context in the study of development has been common for some time. Bronfenbrenner (1979) has been one of the leading proponents of the view that developmentalists have been claiming generality for observations gathered in highly restricted contexts, and has made the often quoted statement that "developmental psychology, as it now exists, is *the science of the strange behavior of children in strange situations with strange adults for the briefest possible periods of time"* (p. 19, italics in original).

It is interesting to note, however, that Bronfenbrenner's examples and analyses have generally concentrated on studies of social interaction. For instance, Bronfenbrenner (1979) discussed studies comparing patterns of parent-infant and parent-child interaction in the laboratory and at home. He presented evidence that findings regarding social class differences in interaction appear to be specific to the use of a strange observational setting or to the presence of an observer and that the same may be true for differences between daycare- and home-reared children. Similarly, he noted that frequency and patterns of help-giving may be different in the laboratory and on the street, and that intellectual testing of disadvantaged children in different contexts may produce different results.

Another indication of concern for the effects of context, this time specifically with regard to cognitive development, may be seen in the approach of cross-cultural psychologists who have led a movement to view cultural variables as vital to the results obtained in experiments (Laboratory of Comparative Human Cognition, 1979). For instance, Rogoff (in press) found that poor story recall among Mayan, as compared with American children, could easily be expained as due to the fact that children were asked to retell a story, told to them by one adult, to another adult. This contradicted a cultural value that children should not presume to tell adults information but should rather defer to their superiority. To maintain social appropriateness, children frequently interjected the word "cha" into their stories. This word means "so I have been told" and was used to make clear that the child was not presuming to claim knowledge of the story for him- or herself.

Although the examples offered by Bronfenbrenner and by the cross-cultural psychologists are striking, the fact that these examples involve social interactions, issues of social class, and comparisons between groups which differ fairly obviously in culture and context has, I suspect, made many investigators concerned with cognitive developmental phenomena feel somewhat secure from the criticism that their results may not be generalizable outside the laboratory. This is despite the fact that cross-cultural and developmental psychology "are each engaged in comparing the performances of different groups: in one case, people of different cultures; in the other, children of different ages" (Laboratory of Comparative Human Cognition, 1979, p. 828).

Clear demonstrations of the importance of affective and social variables for cognitive developmental work are thus vital in convincing laboratory researchers to consider seriously what effect their procedures have on their data. Acredolo's findings (Chapter Two) regarding the importance of emotional factors in the study of the infant's spatial knowledge provide one such example. Acredolo finds that nine-month-olds, when they feel secure in an environment, are able to demonstrate an ability to make objective rather than egocentric searches for objects. This is in contrast to her own earlier data (1978) showing egocentric searches when six- and eleven-month-old infants were tested in laboratory environments without prior experience designed to produce emotional security.

Acredolo's demonstration of nonegocentric choice in children as young as nine months, under the proper conditions, shows that the mean level of performance possible has been underestimated in nine-month-olds, that is, that their competence is greater than was formerly thought. The finding may or may not show that the magnitude of age-related change between nine and sixteen months has been correspondingly overestimated; assessing this proposition would require testing older children also under conditions of emotional security. It may be that sequences of development of spatial cognition are constant, although the age at which particular levels are reached depends on the familiarity of the context of testing. On the other hand, perhaps familiarity has a greater impact on the younger infants than the older ones, so that age-related change in this age range is observed only in unfamiliar environments.

All of these questions are of course matters for further research. What has already been shown by Acredolo, however, is that issues of context are important ones for the study of the development of spatial cognition as for the rest of developmental psychology. In particular, much reevaluation will be needed of research in which children of various ages learn about spatial layouts in an unfamiliar setting and then are tested for their spatial knowledge. Conclusions about lack of particular competencies in younger populations may possibly depend on differential anxiety in the strange situation on the part of the younger subjects.

Cohen (Chapter Four) reports a study which also links research on spatial cognition to issues of ecological validity in developmental research in general. This study concerned whether the context in which spatial information is acquired influences later spatial memory. In particular, do children perform better when memory is a means to a goal than when memory is a goal in itself, as proposed in the Soviet memory literature (Meacham, 1977)? The study in fact showed that an "interact/linked" condition, in which children learned a space in a meaningful context of preparing to mail a letter, facilitated children's distance estimations. This study is very reminiscent of a study of free recall by Istomina (1975) in which she found superior performance when the list of to-be-recalled words was presented to the children as a grocery list, with a model store available for them to make purchases later.

The letter-mailing study shows that young children's spatial knowledge, as well as their abilities, may often be underestimated when they are asked to perform in typical laboratory situations, where the only reason for performance is to please the experimenter or to demonstrate their intelligence. In this connection, however, it is interesting to note that first and sixth graders in the Cohen study benefited equivalently from participating in the interact/linked condition. This suggests that, at least within this age range, it may *not* be true that motivational problems or difficulty in understanding the purpose of the experimental task are the cause of apparent age-related differences in the accuracy of distance estimation, since younger children do not appear differentially subject to these motivational problems.

Measures and Conclusions. Both Liben and Cohen (this volume) discuss the need for multiple dependent measures in the study of spatial cognition and the need to talk about precisely specified spatial competencies in the plural, rather than about spatial competence in the singular, unless converging measures point to a singular conclusion about the nature of spatial representation. The need for convergent measurement is, of course, a familiar theme in psychology, as familiar as the need to consider the generalizability of findings across contexts. But, like the need to consider the social and emotional context of the laboratory experiment, it is a message more honored in the breach than in the observance. The resistance to both is not accidental, since both entail the use of designs considerably more complex than those now in use, as well as the reevaluation of accumulated knowledge. The convergent measurement issue is especially troublesome in that, if different measures do not agree, as they did not in Newcombe and Liben (in press), we seem forced to talk about spatial representations in the plural, and are faced with the question of how many such representations of a single spatial layout there could, in principle, be, and how our consideration of them could be grouped in such a way that we could arrive at illuminating generalizations about either spatial cognition or development.

The fear that adopting multiple dependent measures in the study of spatial cognition is opening the door to a multiplicity of confusing findings surely deters experimenters from using them. But the implicit assumption is that different methods of asking about memory ought to lead straightforwardly to the same conclusions about the nature of spatial representations, in the same way as different means of assessing an attitude or personality trait ought to agree if measures are to be considered convergently valid and if traits and attitudes are to be considered to exist. But the verbal memory literature has long recognized that different methods of asking about memory do not lead to the same answers; that, for instance, subjects recognize low frequency words better than high frequency words, but the opposite is true for recall (for example, Glanzer and Bowles, 1976). The reasons for the difference are not fully resolved (Mandler, 1980), but certainly no one believes a dilemma is posed by the recognition-recall difference regarding whether the subject does or does not have a determinate memory trace. Rather we believe that a representation exists, but this is paired with a set of mental processes for addressing the task in question, which in combination generate the observed behavior (Anderson, 1978). A much needed step in the area of spatial cognition is to develop and test models pairing hypothesized spatial representations with mental processes which act upon these representations when certain tasks must be accomplished. We cannot regard the fact that different methods for tapping spatial representations seem to lead to different results simply as a disturbing nuisance; the phenomenon is, rather, of great intrinsic interest, a point of departure for further work.

Stage and Sequence in the Development of Spatial Cognition

With the possible exception of the question of nature versus nurture, no question in developmental psychology has a longer history or a more conceptually convoluted framework than that of whether development is continuous or discontinuous, stage-like or not, quanititative or qualitative (see, for example, Lerner, 1976). In Liben's chapter, she reminds us of the pendulums of fashion in developmental psychology concerning whether children are seen as basically competent until proven otherwise and liable to have their abilities underestimated by adult researchers (a "child advocacy" approach), or whether children's thought is assumed to be limited in many ways and fundamentally different from the thought of adults. This pendulum, of course, affects all cognitive developmentalists not just those interested in spatial cognition. There is a correlated pendulum, perhaps less noticeable, concerning the efficiency and maturity attributed to adult cognition; researchers can emphasize the imperfections and mistakes in adult thought, or, especially by way of contrast with the thought of children, emphasize its power and elegance.

Recent efforts have been made in many areas of cognitive developmental research to demonstrate the competence of very young children on various tasks, especially Piagetian ones, when the requirements are in some way simplified. For instance, there have been studies to show that young children can correctly answer class inclusion questions if: (1) the "class" referred to is a collection ("army", "flock") rather than a category ("flowers") (Markman and Seibert, 1976); (2) the "class" referred to is marked by inclusion of an adjective true of all members ("sleeping cows"), rather than the class being simply the unmodified term ("cows"), (McGarrigle, Grieve, and Hughes, 1978); (3) the "class" referred to has a distinctive perceptual feature ("houses with windows") (Wilkinson, 1976). Studies of this sort tend to suggest that development is more continuous in nature than Piaget generally seems to suppose, with levels of performance increasing with age due to increases in ability to cope with tricky questions or with increasing complexity, increasing time delays, decreasing degrees of contextual relevance, or the like. Those who favor a more discontinuous view can counter with studies to show that apparently mature behavior on the part of young children is due to an artifact of methodology and not to true understanding; see Dean, Chabaud, and Bridges (1981) for demonstrations of this sort with regard to Markman and Seibert's and Wilkinson's work on class inclusion.

To the extent that young children can be shown to succeed on tasks much earlier than was formerly thought, structural stage theories are brought into question, not because particular age norms have been shown to be incorrect, but because the amount of "horizontal decalage" possibly present in the system has been increased. To put the same point another way, demonstrations of the logical competencies of the very young in certain simple situations are demonstrations of the measurement problems of which Flavell (1971) has written very clearly. What measurement is to count as a measure of a certain logical competence, whose relationship to other abilities (for instance, their sequentiality or concurrence) is to be assessed?

A symmetric point can be made with respect to demonstrations of adult lack of competence, although this tack is less common in the continuous versus discontinuous development controversy. That is, if adults can be shown to resemble children, for instance, when confronting novel situations or dealing with large amounts of information, it is hard to conclude that adults' thought considered as a whole is or is not in a particular stage, does or does not possess a particular structure. Rather, it begins to seem that both adults and children may have similar logical competencies, and that the limitations on the performance of the children are simply more frequent and more severe.

There is an interesting difference here between the structural developmental theory of Piaget and Werner's theory of differentiation and hierarchic integration. These theories are often grouped together under the heading of organismic theories, but one difference is that Werner explicitly considered the possibility of a parallel between the development of thought in new situations (microgenesis in the thought of people of any age) and development of thought with age (ontogenesis). An implication of this view is that sequences of development, as Feldman (1980) has argued, may be invariant, and even stage-like but may be specific to domains of knowledge. In this view, a person can be considered as in a stage only if the domain of knowledge is specified. A further needed specification may be the complexity of the task; Fischer (1980) has developed this point in expounding what he calls *skill theory* and has attempted to specify how complexity could be defined in terms of *a priori* task analyses of tasks within particular domains.

These issues are of course exceedingly complex. What I will do in the rest of this chapter is to consider three, not mutually exclusive, characterizations of how children change with age in their performance of spatial tasks. These accounts are stage-like in nature and based, to varying degrees, on Piaget's ideas—transition from topological to Euclidean frames of reference; the construction of configurational, as well as landmark and route, knowledge; acquisition of conservation of distance and length. (A fourth stage-like account, that children change with age in their reliance on functional, or action-based, distance for estimating distance, will not be discussed for lack of space, and because comments on this progression can be found in the chapters by Cohen and Liben.) More quantitative or continuous explanations of development in spatial cognition stress processes such as: increases with age in integrative processing capacity; acquisition of strategies for dealing with spatial tasks; accumulation of environmental experience (in general, and with specific environments). For each subsection, I will summarize some of the relevant data supporting the existence of age-related change along that dimension. I will also present for each area some evidence regarding whether adults, under some conditions, continue to make childish mistakes in dealing with spatial tasks and whether children, under some conditions, can show adult spatial competence.

Topological to Euclidean Frames of Reference. Piaget and Inhelder (1956) describe young children as possessing only topological concepts of space, that is, concepts which permit the encoding of locations as next to one another or not, contained within one another or not, but which do not allow encoding of location using a reference system which is independent of landmarks and metric in nature. Acquistion of such a Euclidean system is said to take place in later childhood.

There has been a recent claim that Euclidean reference systems can be demonstrated, not only in very young children, but even in a child born blind. Specifically, Landau, Gleitman, and Spelke (1981) present evidence regarding the ability of a two and a half-year-old blind child to walk to locations, when the routes walked were never directly presented to her during training. Her behavior does not seem to demonstrate a precise knowledge of angular displacement, however, since the procedure, dependent variable, and analysis were flawed in a variety of ways. (See Liben and Newcombe in this volume for a critique of the methodology and conclusions.)

Aside from this recent work, there have not been efforts to claim Euclidean knowledge for the young child. What of the Euclidean knowledge of the adult? In the literature on large-scale cognition, assessment of the hypothesized shift from topological to Euclidean frames of reference has generally involved examining the relative reliance of children of different ages on the presence of landmarks to encode spatial location accurately. For instance, Acredolo, Pick, and Olsen (1975) found that three- and four-year-olds, but not eight-year-olds, performed better at locating a bunch of dropped keys in a differentiated rather than an undifferentiated environment. *Differentiation* in this study referred to the presence of a chair in an unfamiliar hallway. Herman and Siegel (1978) found that kindergarten children had particular difficulty, as compared to children from grades two and five, in learning the locations of buildings in a model village when the village was located in a large, relatively undifferentiated gymnasium. This problem did not appear when the village was located in a smaller, more differentiated classroom. Liben, Moore, and Golbeck (in press) found that preschoolers performed better in placing bounded items (those bordering on permanent landmarks) than unbounded items (those not adjacent to landmarks).

In the Liben, Moore, and Golbeck study, adults did not show a difference between performance with bounded and unbounded items, but this may have been because their performances were virtually perfect on all trials; in fact, Liben, Moore, and Golbeck did not evaluate the adult data statistically for this reason. It is possible that adults might have shown an unbounded versus bounded item difference if tested, for example, in an unfamiliar environment in which all placements were less accurate. In this regard, it should also be noted that ceiling effects may account in part for the performance of the eight-year-olds in the study by Acredolo, Pick, and Olsen, and for the significant age by "differentiation" interaction of that study. In short, support for the idea that older children and adults are less dependent than younger children on the presence of landmarks is fairly sparse, since older subjects have rarely been tested in such a way as to push their capabilities and reveal potential limitations. The fact that kindergarteners learned spatial positions very slowly in the gymnasium used by Herman and Siegel (1978) remains an intriguing fact supporting the idea that young children may be especially reliant on the presence of nearby landmarks for spatial coding.

Another kind of evidence for a topological-to-Euclidean shift in large-scale spatial cognition has been provided by Allen (see Chapter Three). Allen found developmental improvement in solving distance problems involving locations within the same subdivision of a route, at least for one of two intrasubdivision tasks. For intrasubdivision problems, metric knowledge is required because subjects cannot arrive at a solution simply by using facts regarding whether or not locations are in the same subdivision.

It is important to note, however, that both Allen's work, and the research of Maki (1981) and Stevens and Coupe (1978) with adults only, suggest the importance of categorization and clustering in adults' memory for spatial location and adults' lack of use of accurate computational systems in many cases. Reliance on categorization is essentially use of the topological concept of neighbourhood. Accurate (or fairly accurate) estimation of metric distance is seen only within categories and clusters.

Allen suggests that adults are trading accuracy for savings in effort by relying on knowledge of which locations belong to which clusters in cases where this is possible. That is, adults could be metrically accurate even on intersubdivision problems but they don't bother. However, this remains to be shown directly, for example, by giving adults incentives to demonstrate accurate metric knowledge across subdivisions. In the absence of such data, it is possible that Allen's finding basically reflects improvement with age at making distance estimates in cases where categorization does not induce distortion. But there is no evidence from his study that children are more susceptible than adults to categorization effects, or more exclusively reliant on subdivision membership in making judgments.

Nelson and Chaiklin (1980) have recently shown evidence of adult reliance on the topological concepts of near and not near for spatial coding in a small-scale spatial memory task. Subjects were asked to reproduce the location of dots located on the radii of a circle which contained smaller concentric circles. There was evidence that they remembered the dots basically as near or not near the circles and misplaced dots so as to be nearer to the circle landmarks than they actually were. Whether or not such effects would obtain in an analogous large-scale task was not assessed. However, in a large-scale study in which adults had to learn twenty locations, in a space divided by opaque and transparent barriers (Liben and Newcombe, in preparation; see Liben, Chapter Five), adults asked to place discs on a piece of cardboard to make a map of the space were significantly more accurate for locations close to the barriers (which may be considered landmarks) and less accurate for locations further from the barriers. The correlation between amount of error in placement and distance of the location from the nearest barrier was .69.

The topological-to-Euclidean shift may best be conceptualized as a shift from a cognitive system in which only topological concepts are available, to a system in which spatial coordinates can be understood and are, in fact, used in certain cases. However, adults certainly do not use coordinates in all cases, and one challenge for future research is to specify under what conditions this occurs. Specifically, do the adult errors relate to an effort-accuracy tradeoff, as Allen suggests, or are coordinate systems simply too difficult to use in certain contexts (for example, large-scale spaces, many locations, impoverished stimuli surrounds) no matter what the motivation? One possibility is that, with age, people become better at using distant, as well as near, landmarks to encode spatial location; this would increase accuracy and decrease apparent reliance on neighboring landmarks, without involving use of true metric coordinates.

Configurational Knowledge, Commutativity, and Transitive Inference. Siegel and White (1975) proposed that children progress from learning landmarks (the distinctive items in the terrain), to learning routes which connect these landmarks, to integrating information about routes to form an overall representation something like a survey map, but perhaps better termed *configurational knowledge.* (See Downs, 1981, for a discussion of the dangers of using map metaphors in studies of spatial knowledge.) Curtis, Siegel, and Furlong (1981) provide evidence that configurational knowledge improves developmentally in the elementary school years, while landmark and route knowledge, in a familiar environment, show fewer age-related differences.

There are at least two skills which seem necessary to the formation of configurational knowledge (although a prerequisite relationship has not yet been empirically demonstrated). One is commutativity, or the understanding that the distance from A to B must be the same as the distance from B to A. In this context, it is interesting to note that adults do not always observe commutativity in making distance judgments (Sadalla, Burroughs, and Staplin, 1980). Sadalla, Burroughs, and Staplin have shown that noncommutativity arises when one location is a salient landmark or reference point and the other location is a less salient place, apparently encoded with respect to the landmark. In this case, the nonreference point is judged closer to the reference point than the reference point is to the nonreference point. It would be interesting to have equivalent data on the judgments of children, since children may be more susceptible than adults to such errors. However, the fact that adults exhibit such distortions at all serves to demonstrate that an attribution of precise computational accuracy and freedom from seemingly illogical judgments to adults would be unwise.

A second skill which may be important to the acquisition of configurational knowledge is transitive inference as applied to spatial positions. An example may be taken from Hazen, Lockman, and Pick (1978) who used arrays of small rooms, explored either in a U-or Z-shaped path, to examine children's ability to make spatial inferences. Each room contained a toy animal. Using children in the age range of three to six years, Hazen, Lockman and Pick found that understanding of the route, and of the sequence of animals along the route, improved with age but that the ability to make spatial inferences (that is, to anticipate what animals would be seen if doors were opened which had not originally been explored) was quite poor at all ages. Knowing that straight ahead from the lion is the elephant and that the bear is a right turn from the elephant and that the cow is to the right of the bear is not sufficient, for these young children, to allow the inference that the cow is to the right of the lion.

This kind of spatial inference seems even more difficult than the transitive inference generally assessed in developmental research, involving, for instance, sticks longer and shorter than each other (for instance, Bryant and Trabasso, 1971; Youniss and Murray, 1970). There are proposals that transitivity problems are solved by construction of a spatial array (see, Huttenlocher, 1968). But such an array is along one spatial dimension (that is, in a straight line) whereas the terms of comparison in the case of large-scale spatial cognition (right, left, ahead, 45° to the right) are such that constructing an array requires use of two dimensions. This is a coordinate space, and returns us to the topological-to-Euclidean transition discussed in the previous section. To acquire configurational knowledge through transitive inference in a large-scale spatial task, one must not only code individual items with respect to a coordinate system but also be able to use these coordinate codings to compute the orientation and distance of items with respect to each other, even when the connection between them has not been directly experienced.

There is little work on whether young children can, in some cases, make spatial inferences of this sort, but there is a large literature on children's ability to make transitive inferences of the classic kind. Trabasso (1975, 1977) and Bryant (1974) have claimed that preschoolers can solve transitivity problems if proper steps are taken to assure that they understand the task and remember the premise material. (However, see Breslow, 1981, for a conceptual and methodological critique.) The research by Bryant and Trabasso suggests that work should be done to examine children's ability to make spatial inferences in cases where they have been trained to a high criterion on memory for the premise information. Children in the Hazen, Lockman, and Pick study did remember the directly experienced links fairly well, but there was variability in this and certainly not a ceiling or criterion performance.

With regard to the performance of older subjects on transitive inference, there are examples in the literature of adults failing to make transitive inferences when learning verbal information, at least when this requires the combination of new premise information with real-world knowledge in a laboratory situation (Potts, Keller, and Rooley, 1981). Are there corresponding limitations on adults' ability to draw spatial inferences and construct configurations? Indeed, Evans, Marrero, and Butler (1981) found that, when encountering new environments, adults initially form fragmented representations consisting of landmarks arrayed in order within clusters and with clusters in order with respect to each other. Over time, landmarks become better linked by routes, and Euclidean measures of accuracy improve. But adult sketch maps, even of familiar environments, are still very likely to contain errors, such as representing intersections as 90° (even when they deviate markedly from that angle) or straightening crooked boundaries (Tversky, 1981).

The Evans, Marrero, and Butler study suggests the possibility that children's apparent lack of configurational knowledge could be due, at least in part, to their limited and often passive exposure to many environments. Hart (1981) certainly found examples of cases in which children given unusual amounts and kinds of environmental experience seemed to be able to construct surprisingly configurational models of their home town. Further work on this issue, using more quantitative criteria and larger samples of children, is clearly needed.

Conservation of Distance and Length. Although conservation of distance and length have their place in Piaget's description of the transition to concrete operations, these abilities are rarely discussed or assessed in the context of research on large-scale spatial cognition (but see Liben, 1980, who also describes our own pilot work in this area). Thus, progression from preoperational to concrete operational status on these dimensions does not have the same status as do the topological-to-Euclidean or landmark-route-configuration hypotheses. But the lack of consideration of these operative abilities seems a pity since there are clear similarities between the assessments of conservation of distance and length, typically done in small-scale contexts, with the kinds of judgments required in many studies of knowledge of large-scale space. Conservation of distance involves asking the child whether the distance between two objects (two small trees) stays the same when various physical barriers are introduced between them (a block, a wall, or a fence which can be seen through). The examiner also asks if the distance is the same when a gate in the fence or a door in the wall is opened rather than closed. The conservation of distance procedure is extremely similar to a large-scale experiment conducted by Kosslyn, Pick, and Fariello (1974; see chapters by Cohen and by Liben for details) in which subjects are asked (through rank ordering) about distances between objects separated or not separated by opaque or transparent barriers. There are several differences, however. One, of course, is scale since conservation of distance is a table-top procedure. A second difference is that, in conservation of distance, judgments are made with the items perceptually present rather than remembered. A third difference involves the fact that Kosslyn, Pick, and Fariello used a rank ordering task to assess knowledge rather than a task in which only two items need to be considered at a time.

In spite of, or perhaps because of, these procedural differences, it is intriguing to note that the mistake nonconservers typically make on the conservation of distance task is to say that the trees are no longer the same distance apart when a barrier intervenes, but rather closer because "the wall takes up space." This is a judgment opposite from that which people seem to make in the Kosslyn, Pick, and Fariello study, where children's rank orderings suggest that objects separated by both opaque and transparent barriers are considered further apart when separated by opaque barriers. (However, distance estimates do not show this pattern of distortions; see Newcombe and Liben, in press.) Further research will obviously be necessary to establish the reasons for the apparent contradiction between table-top conservation of distance judgments and representation of large-scale space and the reasons for adult distortion across opaque barriers. But it is hard to believe that the development of conservation of distance is not important to the development of spatial representation; if it is, the study of large-scale spatial cognition will have yet another point of contact with Piagetian stage theory.

The second kind of conservation which seems relevant to spatial cognition is conservation of length. Conservation of length assessments, in one version, involve judgments of the length of lines made of matchsticks. Two arrays are initially shown to be equal in length along a straight line. One array of matchsticks is then rearranged to form a path with turns. Nonconservers then judge it no longer equal to the untransformed line. Typically, they say it is shorter since its end point comes before the end point of the straight line.

This task also has an analogue in the study of large-scale spatial cognition. Sadalla and Magel (1980) have found that adults judge routes with turns longer than straight-line routes even when the distances are in fact equal. (Note again a contrast between the situations: The nonconserving child generally thinks the table-top line with turns is shorter, not longer, than the straight line.) The crucial factor adding difficulty to the judgments made by adults in the Sadalla and Magel situation is probably the fact that the distances are never directly experienced as equal prior to a transformation. Thus, strictly speaking, the experiment does not deal with the phenomenon of conservation since conservation involves the understanding that perceptual transformations cannot destroy known equalities. It would be interesting to know, however, if distortions also occur when adults initially walk straight-line routes and then traverse the same routes deformed into zig-zags. Would the added effort involved in turning cause them to increase their distance estimations? Would it cause children to alter their distance estimations? Might developmental differences in conservation of length, in small- and large-scale contexts, be related to other aspects of spatial representation?

Conclusion. There is little evidence that young children encode locations in coordinate space, make spatial inferences to construct configurational knowledge, or conserve distance or length. Thus, at least to date, the age of first appearance of these spatial abilities does not seem to change markedly, depending on the demands of the task, unlike the case of class inclusion. A stage approach to spatial cognition thus does not have to account for demonstrations of unexpected early competence. It is possible, however, that this state of affairs obtains only because the attention of investigators has not been focussed on the issue of age of first appearance, as it has been in areas of research such a class inclusion or transitivity. Acredolo's findings regarding the importance of familiarity in assessments of infants' spatial capabilities, the appearance of the initial work by Landau, Gleitman, and Spelke and the work of Hart on environmental experience, however, all suggest that the race may be on to demonstrate precocious achievement of several of these capabilities.

However, there is some evidence that adults do not always encode locations in coordinate spaces or infer configurational knowledge and may not even conserve distance and length in large-scale spatial tasks. Whether this is due to an effort-accuracy tradeoff, to the use in experiments of novel environments (which may not be completely encoded), or to limitations on adult thought when large quantities of information must be considered simultaneously is not known. The fact, however, that adulthood does not represent an endpoint of development in which performance on spatial tasks is imposingly logical and error free must be recognized.

Research in large-scale spatial cognition has been more focussed, generally, than other cognitive developmental research on issues of sequence than of stage, sequences which have generally been internal to the domain of knowledge considered (namely, large-scale space). This has the advantage, perhaps, of having avoided much of the agonizing about the existence of stages considered as structures in the person which has occurred in the rest of the study of cognitive development. We have been able to consider quite happily the existence of parallels between ontogenesis and microgenesis (as when adults encounter a new environment), and this has generated many interesting studies. Research on spatial cognition in the future, however, may have to grapple with relating changes in spatial representation and thought to other cognitive developmental changes, such as the development of transitive inference and the acquisition of conservation. This will involve confronting some of the issues of stage which have to date been avoided. Research will also, I think, have to address the issues of whether children are wholly incapable of using coordinate systems or constructing configurational knowledge (or whether they can show these competencies in certain favorable situations) and of why adults seem embarrassingly prone to show category-induced distortions in spatial judgments rather than use coordinate systems or to rely on representations of novel environments including landmarks arrayed in an ordinally, but not metrically, correct manner. This will mean facing squarely the issue of whether descriptions of development in spatial cognition are meant to be structural stage theories or not.

Summary

The theme of this chapter has been that researchers in spatial cognition are more part of the mainstream of cognitive developmental research than it has sometimes seemed in the past decade. We confront the same methodological issues (choices of context, choices of dependent variable) and the same conceptual problems in describing the nature of developmental change. The development of spatial cognition is only a part of cognitive development and must be linked to it. One of the unique aspects of research on spatial representation, however, may be that people so frequently encounter and learn about new environments. This offers the potential for looking in detail at questions of the extent to which microgenesis and ontogenesis are similar and of the nature of the resemblance of adult and child thought.

References

Acredolo, L. P. "Development of Spatial Orientation in Infancy." *Developmental Psychology,* 1978, *14,* 224–234.

Acredolo, L. P., Pick, H. L., and Olsen, M. G. "Environmental Differentiation and Familiarity as Determinants of Children's Memory for Spatial Location." *Developmental Psychology,* 1975, *11,* 495–501.

Anderson, J. R. "Arguments Concerning Representations for Mental Imagery." *Psychological Review,* 1978, *85,* 249–277.

Breslow, L. "Reevaluation of the Literature on the Development of Transitive Inferences." *Psychological Bulletin,* 1981, *89,* 325–351.

Bronfenbrenner, U. *The Ecology of Human Development.* Cambridge: Harvard University Press, 1979.

Bryant, P. E. *Perception and Understanding in Young Children.* New York: Basic Books, 1974.

Bryant, P. E., and Trabasso, T. "Transitive Inferences and Memory in Young Children." *Nature,* 1971, *232,* 456–458.

Curtis, L. E., Siegel, A. W., and Furlong, N. E. "Developmental Differences in Cognitive Mapping: Configurational Knowledge of Familiar Large-Scale Environments." *Journal of Experimental Child Psychology,* 1981, *31,* 456–469.

Dean, A. L., Chabaud, S., and Bridges, E. "Classes, Collections, and Distinctive Features: Alternative Strategies for Solving Inclusion Problems." *Cognitive Psychology,* 1981, *13,* 84–112.

Downs, R. M. "Maps and Mappings as Metaphors for Spatial Representation." In L. S. Liben, A. H. Patterson, and N. Newcombe (Eds.), *Spatial Representation and Behavior Across the Life Span.* New York: Academic Press, 1981.

Evans, G. W., Marrerro, D. G., and Butler, P. A. "Environmental Learning and Cognitive Mapping." *Environment and Behavior,* 1981, *13,* 83–104.

Feldman, D. H. *Beyond Universals in Cognitive Development.* Norwood, N.J.: Ablex, 1980.

Fischer, K. W. "A Theory of Cognitive Development: The Control and Construction of Hierarchies of Skills." *Psychological Review,* 1980, *87,* 477–531.

Flavell, J. H. "Stage Related Properties of Cognitive Development." *Cognitive Psychology,* 1971, *2,* 421–453.

Glanzer, M., and Bowles, N. "Analysis of the Word Frequency Effect in Recognition Memory." *Journal of Experimental Psychology: Human Learning and Memory,* 1976, *2,* 21–31.

Hart, R. A. "Children's Spatial Representation of the Landscape: Lessons and Questions from a Field Study." In L. S. Liben, A. H. Patterson, and N. Newcombe (Eds.), *Spatial Representation and Behavior Across the Life Span.* New York: Academic Press, 1981.

Hazen, N. L., Lockman, J. J., and Pick, H. L. "The Development of Children's Representations of Large-Scale Environments." *Child Development,* 1968, *49,* 623–636.

Herman, J. F., and Siegel, A. W. "The Development of Cognitive Mapping of the Large-Scale Environment." *Journal of Experimental Child Psychology,* 1978, *26,* 389–401.

Huttenlocher, J. "Constructing Spatial Images: A Strategy in Reasoning." *Psychological Review,* 1968, *75,* 550–560.

Istomina, Z. M. "The Development of Voluntary Memory in Preschool-Age Children." *Soviet Psychology,* 1975, *13,* 5-64.

Kosslyn, S. M., Pick, H. L., and Fariello, G. R. "Cognitive Maps in Children and Men." *Child Development,* 1974, *45,* 707-716.

Laboratory of Comparative Human Cognition. "Cross-Cultural Psychology's Challenges to our Ideas of Children and Development." *American Psychologist,* 1979, *34,* 827-833.

Landau, B., Gleitman, H., and Spelke, E. "Spatial Knowledge and Geometric Representation in a Child Blind from Birth." *Science,* 1981, *213,* 1275-1278.

Lerner, R. M. *Concepts and Theories of Human Development.* Reading, Mass.: Addison-Wesley, 1976.

Liben, L. S. "The Effect of Operativity on Memory." Paper presented to the Southeastern Conference on Human Development, Alexandria, Va., April 1980.

Liben, L. S., Moore, M. M., and Golbeck, S. L. "Preschoolers' Knowledge of Their Classroom Environment: Evidence from Small-Scale and Life-Size Spatial Tasks." *Child Development,* in press.

Liben, L. S., and Newcombe, N. "Inferring Spatial Knowledge in a Young Blind Child." Submitted for publication, 1981.

Maki, R. H. "Categorization and Distance Effects with Spatial Linear Orders." *Journal of Experimental Psychology: Human Learning and Memory,* 1981, *7,* 15-32.

Mandler, G. "Recognizing: The Judgment of Previous Occurrence." *Psychological Review,* 1980, *87,* 252-271.

Markman, E., and Seibert, J. "Classes and Collections: Internal Organization and Resulting Holistic Properties." *Cognitive Psychology,* 1976, *8,* 561-577.

McGarrigle, J., Grieve, R., and Hughes, M. "Interpreting Inclusion: A Contribution to the Study of the Child's Cognitive and Linguistic Development." *Cognitive Psychology,* 1978, *26,* 528-550.

Meacham, J. "Soviet Investigations of Memory Development." In R. V. Kail and J. W. Hagen (Eds.), *Perspectives on the Development of Memory and Cognition.* Hillsdale, N.J.: Erlbaum, 1977.

Nelson, T. O., and Chaiklin, S. "Immediate Memory for Spatial Location." *Journal of Experimental Psychology: Human Learning and Memory,* 1980, *6,* 529-545.

Newcombe, N., and Liben, L. S. "Barrier Effects in the Cognitive Maps of Children and Adults." *Journal of Experimental Child Psychology,* 1982, in press.

Piaget, J., and Inhelder, B. *The Child's Conception of Space.* New York: Norton, 1967.

Potts, G. R., Keller, R. A., and Rooley, C. J. "Factors Affecting the Use of World Knowledge to Complete a Linear Ordering." *Journal of Experimental Psychology: Human Learning and Memory,* 1981, *7,* 254-268.

Rogoff, B. "Approaches to Integrating Context and Cognitive Development." In M. E. Lamb and A. L. Brown (Eds.), *Advances in Developmental Psychology.* Vol. 2. Hillsdale, N.J.: Erlbaum, in press.

Sadalla, E. K., Burroughs, W. J., and Staplin, L. J. "Reference Points in Spatial Cognition." *Journal of Experimental Psychology: Human Learning and Memory,* 1980, *6,* 516-528.

Sadalla, E. K., and Magel, S. G. "The Perception of Traversed Distance." *Environment and Behavior,* 1980, *12,* 65-79.

Siegel, A. W., and White, S. H. "The Development of Spatial Representations of Large-Scale Environments." In H. W. Reese (Ed.), *Advances in Child Development and Behavior.* Vol. 10. New York: Academic Press, 1975.

Stevens, A., and Coupe, P. "Distortions in Judged Spatial Relations." *Cognitive Psychology,* 1978, *10,* 422-437.

Tolman, E. C. "Cognitive Maps in Rats and Men." *Psychological Review,* 1948, *55,* 189-208.

Trabasso, T. "The Role of Memory as a System in Making Transitive Inferences." In R. V. Kail and J. W. Hagen (Eds.), *Perspectives on the Development of Memory and Cognition.* Hillsdale, N.J.: Erlbaum, 1977.

Tversky, B. "Distortions in Memory for Maps." *Cognitive Psychology,* 1981, *13,* 407–433.

Werner, H. *Comparative Psychology of Mental Development.* New York: International Universities Press, 1948.

Wilkinson, A. "Counting Strategies and Semantic Analysis as Applied to Class Inclusion." *Cognitive Psychology,* 1976, *8,* 64–85.

Nora Newcombe is an associate professor of psychology at Temple University. She received her doctorate from Harvard University, and was formerly on the faculty of the Pennsylvania State University. Her research interests are in developmental changes in spatial cognition and in sex differences in spatial ability.

*In this chapter, a new functionalism is offered as a theoretical
alternative for understanding cognitive development. Social functioning
and purpose are stressed, and adult external criteria as standards
are questioned.*

Toward a Social Ecology of Cognitive Mapping

Alexander W. Siegel

Less than a decade ago, a new enterprise emerged on the theatrical stage of
developmental psychology—the development of cognitive mapping of large-
scale environments. In a sense, the enterprise was not really new; there had
been papers by Trowbridge (1913) and Lord (1941) on the spatial orientation
systems used by school children, and Maier (1936) had examined children's
spatial learning in a large maze, but the early papers did not provoke long-
lasting inquiry. In the mid-1970s, empirical studies by Kosslyn, Pick, and Fariello (1974) and Acredolo, Pick, and Olsen (1975) and theoretical review
papers by Hart and Moore (1973) and Siegel and White (1975) appeared to
renew the enterprise. At the time of this writing, cognitive mapping of large-
scale environments has become an industry. The recent flood of both empirical and theoretical writing about cognitive maps and mapping is much more
than the reinvention of the wheel.

The chapters in this volume represent the state of the art in develop-
mental-psychological research on cognitive mapping of large-scale environments. Each author is a cognitive-developmental psychologist, yet each takes a
slightly different perspective, concerned with somewhat different facets of the
domain. I, too, have been engaged in research in cognitive mapping for several
years. But, rather than presenting additional research within my own pet
paradigms or trying to review the vast literature generated by the industry (see

R. Cohen (Ed.). *New Directions for Child Development: Children's Conceptions of Spatial Relationships,* no. 15.
San Francisco: Jossey-Bass, March 1982.

83

Liben, Patterson, and Newcombe, 1981, for a series of such reviews), in this chapter I will take a somewhat broader perspective and try to sketch out, in rough and preliminary form, a larger theoretical and social context of the cognitive mapping enterprise and what it might become.

Rather than trying to respond critically to many of the provocative issues raised by each author or trying to extract common themes (as Nora Newcombe has artfully done in her chapter), I would like to offer and develop a series of broader issues. Specifically, I will try to "map" cognitive mapping theory and research onto current and future concerns in theory and research on cognitive development. First, I would like briefly to reconsider cognitive development within a functionalist perspective, as a process anchored in time and space, and argue that the most pressing need in research on cognitive and social development is for the development of a theory of situations. Second, I will argue that cognitive mapping is an inherently social process and consider briefly a "motivology" of mapping. Finally, I will consider some relations among cognitive mapping, wayfinding, and metaphors that seem to guide our thinking about what constitutes "adaptive" or "accurate" cognitive-mapping performance. Many of the points I will make are not new; they have been made in other places, by myself and others (see Downs and Siegel, 1981; Siegel, 1981; White and Siegel, 1982). It seems useful, however, to raise these points once again, in the hope that future theory and research in the domain of cognitive mapping will be glimpsed through a broader, more ecologically and socially oriented window.

Cognitive Development in Time and Space

Looking at children in the rooms of an experimental laboratory and in the rooms of a school, researchers have most frequently interpreted age changes in learning, memory, cognitive mapping and the like as reflecting mechanisms of cognitive growth and quasi-embryological structural development. But our everyday knowledge (and an implicit assumption in all of this volume's chapters) is that children travel from place to place. Cognitive changes in growing children depend, in large measure, on the functional needs imposed on them during this process of travel and by the requirements of cooperation with people — proximally and distally — that children experience as they enter adult society. Recently, Sheldon White and I (White and Siegel, 1981) have discussed the cognitive development of children moving among natural contexts of human interaction across space and time. In discussing cognitive development in this way, we needed to question and modify some recent assumptions about just what cognitive development is and what the study of cognitive development should entail.

During the last twenty years, structural models of cognitive competence have been the core focus of the central research issues of cognitive development. It has been argued that the structural development of competence must be adaptive, but such arguments have been pretty vague about adaptation for *what*. With some exceptions, the research movements of the last decade have not seriously attempted to explore those contexts towards which adaptation is directed. Life is not primarily a matter of getting along in experimental rooms or school classrooms — the two places in which the study of cognitive development has traditionally taken place — or even in navigable small-scale spaces (see the chapter by Weatherford in this volume). We need a new functionalism that must include, in some broad sense, an analysis and a theory of the contexts of children's behavior.

Contemporary research on child development is a response to the new necessities of modern societies and their new behavior settings (Siegel and White, 1982). For twentieth century American children, it is doubtful that any single kind of environment should be regarded as natural, privileged, or particularly authentic for the specification of a child's psychology (White, 1980). Is a tachistoscope or the layout of a town on the floor of a gymnasium less natural to a child than Sunday school or clarinet lessons? Is a classroom any less natural than Friday night dinner at Aunt Shirley's? What seems obvious is that children live in many situations, and a statement about or a characterization of a child may not automatically hold across any pair of them. A line of theorists from John Dewey (1902) to Kurt Lewin (1935) to Roger Barker (1968; Barker and Wright, 1954) to Michael Cole (Cole, Hood, and McDermott, 1979) to Urie Bronfenbrenner (1979) has argued that a naturalistic developmental psychology can only be achieved through the creation and use of an analysis and theory of situations.

With minor exceptions, the contexts in which children live are social contexts. We abstract the cognitive part of a social adaptation at some peril to the texture and meaning of the cognitive phenomena (a point implicit in Cohen's and Acredolo's chapters in this volume). To understand cognitive development in time and space, we need to understand it as being deeply embedded in a social world, one full of occasions, formalities, and etiquettes (Douglas, 1973).

Notions of a generic socialization are linked with traditional notions of a generic cognitive development. Socialization is often treated as a universal process through which a common stock of knowledge, beliefs, and social forms are acquired by all children in a society. But this is a superficial view of what happens as a group of age peers find niches and roles in any functioning society. Socialization makes children as different as it makes them alike. In modern society, a child comes to occupy only a portion of the contexts of the town or city, that, nominally, he or she inhabits as a whole. Part of the socialization of each child involves the negotiation of a viable and unique set of social contexts used by and lived in by that child. In this negotiation process, children make different adaptations to different contexts. We see marginal developments of what might best be termed a multiple personality. (For example, the often reported low correlation between parent and teacher ratings of a child on a variety of instruments is probably not, primarily, due to the unreliability of the instruments but, rather, due to the fact that the child at home and the child at school are not entirely the same child.) As children enter adult society, they build, in effect, a set of selves to fit a set of social contexts.

As White and I have argued (White and Siegel, 1981), a properly functional view of cognitive development would envision it as something embedded in a child's movement and travel across the social contexts of a society. Socialization thus encompasses a second kind of travel involving symbols. Children learn to engage — by means of reading, writing, the telephone, and, now, the microcomputer — in cooperative activity with people that are far away in space (when, for example, they talk on the phone to Aunt Sophie in Minneapolis) and time (or read the adventures of Tom Sawyer). The often talked about trend in cognitive development towards more abstraction, decontextualization, or distancing of children's thought (Sigel and Cocking, 1977; Werner and Kaplan, 1963) must be regarded as an expression of the child's increasing capacity for long-range communication and coordination with others and must depend on the fact that we call on the growing child to travel and to think about things at a distance.

Finally, a new functionalism should entail an enlarged view of children's knowledge of self. Moving from one setting to another, a child not only experiences other people in those settings but experiences himself or herself in other settings as well. Multiple adaptation on the part of the young child is surely accompanied by a knowledge about self that directs the child toward some sites of action as good, promising, or secure and away from others that, in the child's experience, have proved threatening (see Acredolo, 1981, and her chapter in this volume).

Travel and Cognitive Mapping in a Social World

What do we know about where children travel? In their classic work *Midwest and Its Children* (1954), Barker and Wright studied children in and among the settings of a midwestern American town. They give us views of children that permit us to estimate the ways children travel as they grow up. Barker and Wright seek in their work to lay a foundation for what White and I call a theory of situations. Some general trends are suggested from their carefully collected and massive data. Children spend their earliest years predominantly at home. As children enter school age, they move out into the community; they experience a more differentiated set of psychological environments; they begin to establish secondary "home bases." As children get older they enter more and more centrally into adult community activities to become increasingly central performers.

Although these trends seem obvious, much of this evidence is foreign and challenging to much current theory. Barker and Wright's findings were published nearly thirty years ago. Perhaps developmental psychologists have largely ignored the Midwest work because the findings seem so obvious. Perhaps because of their preoccupations with the learning of free-floating, placeless, decontextualized cues and symbols, developmental psychologists tend to set aside this work. (The early learning theorists debated about "place" versus "response" learning and about "cognitive mapping" [Osgood, 1953] — in fact, it is rather awkward to deal with place and space in a stimulus-response psychology). Piagetian genetic epistemology addresses explicitly the child's construction of time and space, but, as pointed out by a number of the authors in this volume, Piaget's research methods primarily explore children's reactions to a tabletop world of physical phenomena (see also White, 1980).

When children move around in the world, they appear to learn a lot of spatial arrangements around them easily. Allen (this volume) argues that macrospatial knowledge comes so easily to people that we "spatialize" nonspatial things to make them easier to learn — for example, clocks and calendars (Siegel and White, 1975). What do children learn as they travel? Obviously, a child maps a geographical terrain as he or she travels in it: This is a major theme of all of the chapters in the present volume. The child uses a large, quick, recognition-in-context memory to retain images of objects encountered, so that they seem familiar the second time they are seen (Kirasic, Siegel, and Allen, 1980). At the same time, children somehow annotate their retained images so that directions and distances between objects can be estimated (Allen and others, 1979). Using first-order survey maps, which allow them to generate routes never used before, growing children store more and more things and places of their world into their mental stock of known loci (Siegel, Allen, and Kirasic, 1979). The growth of spatial representation — cognitive mapping — in children reflects directly the range and variety of travel that has been permitted to them. For example, Hart (1979) has shown that preschoolers and kindergarteners can produce sophisticated maps — survey maps — of the environs of their home but, at that age, more distal settings are not well represented.

Interestingly, the sequence of actions by which a child produces a map recapitulates, in the world of arranged symbols, some of the pattern of the child's larger encounters with the environment that created the spatial knowledge (using the concept of familiarity as a dependent variable as described in Acredolo's chapter in this volume). Just as children's walking and running ranges out from home base, so does children's map construction. For example, Herman (1980) and Wapner, Kaplan, and Ciottone (1981) have found that when children build maps they start with home; they then put in places that can be seen or easily reached from the home; last they put in less visually and physically accessible places. Hart (1979, 1981) reports that, until about 8½ years of age, children produce dual-level cognitive maps — survey maps of the environs of the home built out with route maps representing fragmentary knowledge picked up in occasional trips out into the world away from home. Without data about the movement and travel of children, such dual-level maps might well be interpreted as instances of structural *decalage*. With data showing that children before the school years spend much time near the home and only occasional time in the larger environment, such maps make another kind of sense. As they gather more and more information about spatial arrangements, children escalate their maps, moving from loosely connected route maps to more complete, more "metric," and more accurate configurational maps (see Allen's and Cohen's chapters in this volume; Curtis, Siegel, and Furlong, 1981).

Maps are not isolated targets of learning in and of themselves. Children remember the places that are meaningful in their everyday lives and note these places as landmarks on the maps they make. Adults point out places of interest as a routine part of preparation for citizenship, wayfinding, hunting and fishing, shopping, and so forth. Adults and children are purposive. The knowledge that people take in on their journeys and the maps they construct selectively enhance those things that seem important to them in the light of their purposes (see the chapter by Cohen in this volume; Siegel, 1981). Relevant to Acredolo's distinctions between intentional and incidental learning and between active and passive experience is the agenda of the traveler. A weekend visitor to a city and a prospective home-buyer will construct maps that probably differ in content, scope, and detail.

Movement and knowledge reciprocally enhance one another in the life of the growing child. Piaget, Inhelder, and Szeminska (1960) recognize this explicitly: "At seven, a child knows several roads; those which take him to school, where he now goes himself, and those which he walks along with his family when they go on their customary walks; he can *therefore* describe several fragmentary routes, and he can draw a plan showing a number of discrete areas. At nine or ten, a child is free as a man and can roam at will all over the town; he *therefore* answers all the questions satisfactorily" (pp. 23–24).

The process of cognitive mapping is only in part cognitive: Children overlay social learning on their cognitive maps. They learn where different behavior settings are and, in so doing, learn where to go to find things, people, personal involvements, or assistance. They learn who the other people are in the community and, in so doing, become aware of the range and extremes of the social, physical, and behavioral differences that people in the community expose to them. They develop normative expectations about social life and social forms. Their social learning involves much more than the simple social attribution mechanisms currently recognized as central issues in social cognition. Children learn how to act properly and skillfully in a number of community behavior settings: Training in style, manner, and etiquette is an integral part of skill training in community settings (such as a department store or the YMCA), just as it is in school and at the family dinner table (Bossard, 1948).

The settings that children experience and subsequently map are by no means randomly chosen. Recently, Whiting (1980) has argued that the power of socializing agents to shape social behavior lies largely in their role in assign-

ment of children to settings. It appears that the most critical features of a setting for developing patterns of social behavior are the actors who occupy the
setting, particularly their age and sex (Munn, 1973; Whiting, 1980).

Children's situational learning also centrally involves attitudinal and
motivational aspects. Community settings differ in the emotional atmospher-
ics they maintain or offer to a child. Barker and Wright (1954) observed Roy
Eddy, a six-year-old, enter seventeen community behavior settings in one day
and receive an interesting variety of greetings: "In some settings Roy was
ignored, restricted, and coerced, but in others he was warmly welcomed,
helped, and given great social approval and self-esteem" (p. 96).

Children also experience changes in tempo in different settings
(Wapner, 1980) and must learn how to manage their own behavior enough to
operate in a setting and be in tune with it. As children pick up the emotional
tones, tempos, and the self-management demands of diverse behavior settings, an emotional overlay appears on their cognitive maps: Which settings
are safe? Which are unsafe? In what settings does the child feel secure? Where
does he or she trust? (See the chapter by Acredolo in this volume.)

Issues of freedom—free movement, autonomy, free will—seem to be
critical aspects of a child's cognitive development and socialization. Barker
and Wright (1954) remark that "The six-year-old had privileges and opportun-
ities not available to the 4-year-old, and the 8-year-old had more freedom,
more status, more power than the 6-year-old" (p. 102). Rogoff and others
(1975) surveyed cross-cultural reports of children's entries into adult roles and
responsibilities in the school years. Mobility, freedom, responsibility, status,
and power seem to rise together as children gradually enter the behavior settings of the adult world. What is the engine that drives this process? Part of it,
surely, is what Robert White (1959) has called a need for competence. But
note that Barker and Wright (1954) allude to the freedom, status, and power
that accrue to the growing child; Piaget, Inhelder, and Szeminska (1960)
speak of the child of nine or ten as "free as a man." Just conceivably, part of
what drives a child to cognitively map the environment and to enter adult
behavior settings in increasingly central, performing roles is his or her need
for freedom and dignity.

The World of the Child and the World According to Rand McNally

For most cognitive and developmental psychologists and geographers,
the cartographic map has been implicitly adopted as the metaphor that guides
our thinking about the structure and function of cognitive maps and shapes
our methodologies for externalizing them (Downs and Siegel, 1981). Further,
the cartographic map is the standard against which performance is typically
compared and then assimilated into hypotheses about cognitive competence.
For the most part, researchers have asked, "To what extent and under what
conditions can adults and children produce models of their environment that

look like cartographic maps (or conform to the properties of cartographic maps)?" The extent to which the models conform to the cartographic maps is assessed in terms of accuracy. Without exception, the word *accuracy* appears in every chapter in the present volume, and in every paper *accuracy* is value-normative — that is, accuracy is considered good and implies being more developed; inaccuracy is bad and implies being less developed.

What is it that is more or less accurate than what? How can we reconcile the apparent paradox between accurate spatial behavior (that is, competent wayfinding) and inaccurate cognitive maps? Clearly, accuracy is agreement with an external standard, but what standard? The real world, of course. From a constructivist metatheoretical position, however, (Pepper, 1970; Reese and Overton, 1970) there is no such thing as the real world. From this perspective, reality is a construction by an individual and by a society. At a number of levels — phylogenetic (Jerison, 1976; von Uexkull, 1957), ontogenetic (Bruner, 1964; Piaget, 1971; Werner, 1957), and sociocultural (Berger and Luckman, 1967; Mead, 1934) — there are multiple real worlds, each of which is a potential standard against which to assess accuracy as agreement (Downs and Siegel, 1981). Further, even if it were possible to reach consensus on a single standard of comparison, the amount of inaccuracy permissable would be a function of the purposes for which the cognitive map is to be used (Wapner, Kaplan, and Cohen, 1973). By acknowledging what Downs (1981) has referred to as *cartographic relativism,* any map — cognitive or cartographic — is a possible world model.

Cartographic maps are but one kind of model — the world according to Rand McNally — in which the world is transformed into a two-dimensional grid in the metric of degrees on abstract axes of latitude and longitude. Yet most of us act and write as if a cartographic map is the best model of reality and as if a cartographic map in the head is the most useful form of knowledge. That is a questionable presupposition.

The primary function of cognitive maps is to facilitate wayfinding in the large-scale environment and to prevent getting lost (Downs and Stea, 1977). Cognitive maps also function as dynamic data stores, as organizers of social and emotional experience, and as devices for inferring novel spatial and nonspatial relationships (Downs and Stea, 1977; Siegel and White, 1975). Surely there are other models of the world, although, perhaps, less elegant and cognitively economical than a cartographic map, that can serve these functions.

In *East Is a Big Bird* (1970), Gladwin describes the navigational system of the Puluwat Islanders; in *We, the Navigators* (1972), Lewis describes the system of the Santa Cruz Islanders. Both of these systems are used in successfully navigating extensive expanses of open ocean. The navigators using these systems do not require compasses, and cartographic maps make little sense to them, yet they never get lost. Clearly, wayfinding in large-scale space can be based on models of the world different from that of the cartographic map, and, just as clearly, cognitive maps in the head need not be cartographic.

Both of these navigational systems (Gladwin, 1970; Lewis, 1972) can be described as home-centered (Trowbridge, 1913) and/or local-reference systems in that those who use them orient themselves with respect to geographic points such as home, an island, a coast, wave formations or other local features (for example, reefs and flights of birds), and to star positions. Such systems are simpleminded (in a nonpejorative sense), practical, and have built in flexibility and redundancy. They involve not terribly elegant algorithms to ensure against getting lost—a consequence of negative adaptive value. These systems require much rote memorization but they are safe. Gatty's (1958) description of home-centered systems is more than faintly reminiscent of the developing child's travel experiences as discussed earlier in this chapter: "As early peoples ventured forth in search of food they maintained a constant anxiety about their home and would often look back to see where they were in relation to their point of departure. Each time they went out more territory would become familiar to them; and they would proceed further . . . never once losing the thread" (p. 46).

In modern, cognitively developed, navigational systems based on the cartographic map, one orients oneself by using astronomically derived bearings such as north and south—often more precisely notated in the metric of degrees—that radiate out from the self. (In a peculiarly interesting sense, such systems might even be termed egocentric.) Such compass-based reference systems are more elegant but riskier. By involving oneself in an intricate system of calculations, whenever one stops to refer to the points of a compass, " . . . he may sever his connection with the previous place. . . . All too easily, in this way, can he lose the thread which tied him to his original place of departure" (Gatty, 1958, p. 47).

Home-centered and local-reference systems have considerable built-in redundancy; thus, they have flexibility and permit the use of multiple strategies. They are conservative in the sense that, while being cumbersome, they also minimize absolutely the possibility of getting lost. Notice further that, frequently, the linguistic descriptions of these systems have much in common with the descriptions of the immature and/or so-called primitive frames of reference attributed to young children by Hart and Moore (1973), Liben (this volume), Piaget (Piaget and Inhelder, 1967), Weatherford (this volume, and Werner (1957). Yet it is clear that these supposedly immature or primitive systems are enormously adaptive and have critical survival value.

In contemporary discussions of cognitive development, competence is frequently defined in "adultomorphic" terms. Thought starts out incompetent in the young child and is said to be competent when it becomes, through a series of unfolding genetic logics, like the thought of adults. One must consider the serious possibility that it is an equally egocentric error to equate competence in cognitive mapping to compass-based navigational systems or the use of abstract, coordinated frames of reference (Hart and Moore, 1973) inherent in cartographic maps. Perhaps we can develop performance as well as competence theories of cognitive mapping by looking at what children do in different contexts and by considering that their models of their multiple worlds may be different from rather than inferior to, the world according to Rand McNally. As I have been arguing throughout this chapter such theories need to be developed within the context of a new functionalism — one in which cognitive development in general and cognitive mapping in particular are viewed as processes embedded in the larger social ecology of the child's world.

References

Acredolo, L. P. "Small- and Large-Scale Spatial Concepts in Infancy and Childhood." In L. S. Liben, A. H. Patterson, and N. Newcombe (Eds.), *Spatial Representation and Behavior Across the Life Span.* New York: Academic Press, 1981.

Acredolo, L. P., Pick, H. L., and Olsen, M. G. "Environmental Differentiation and Familiarity as Determinants of Children's Memory for Spatial Location." *Developmental Psychology,* 1975, *11,* 495–501.

Allen, G. L, Kirasic, K. C., Siegel, A. W., and Herman, J. F. "Developmental Issues in Cognitive Mapping: The Selection and Utilization of Environmental Landmarks." *Child Development,* 1979, *50,* 1062–1070.

Barker, R. G. *Ecological Psychology.* Stanford: Stanford University Press, 1968.

Barker, R. G., and Wright, H. F. *Midwest and Its Children: The Psychological Ecology of an American Town.* Evanston, Ill.: Row, Peterson, 1954.

Berger, P. L., and Luckmann, T. *The Social Construction of Reality.* New York: Anchor, 1967.

Bossard, J. H. S. *The Sociology of Child Development.* New York: Harper, 1948.

Bronfenbrenner, U. *The Ecology of Human Development: Experiments by Nature and Design.* Cambridge: Harvard University Press, 1979.

Bruner, J. S. "The Course of Cognitive Growth." *American Psychologist,* 1964, *19,* 1–15.

Cole, M., Hood, L., and McDermott, R. *Ecological Niche Picking: Ecological Invalidity as an Axiom of Experimental Cognitive Psychology.* New York: Laboratory of Comparative Human Cognition and Institute for Comparative Human Development, Rockfeller University, 1979.

Curtis, L. E., Siegel, A. W., and Furlong, N. E. "Developmental Differences in Cognitive Mapping: Configurational Knowledge of Familiar Large-Scale Environments." *Journal of Experimental Child Psychology,* 1981, *31,* 456–469.

Dewey, J. *The Educational Situation.* Chicago: University of Chicago Press, 1902.

Douglas, M. (Ed.). *Rules and Meanings: The Anthropology of Everyday Knowledge.* New York: Penguin Books, 1973.

Downs, R. M. "Maps and Mappings as Metaphors for Spatial Representation." In L. S. Liben, A. H. Patterson, and N. Newcombe (Eds.), *Spatial Representation and Behavior Across the Life Span.* New York: Academic Press, 1981.

Downs, R. M., and Siegel, A. W. "On Mapping Researchers Mapping Children and Mapping Space." In L. S. Liben, A. H. Patterson, and N. Newcombe (Eds.), *Spatial Representation and Behavior Across the Life Span.* New York: Academic Press, 1981.

Downs, R. M., and Stea, D. *Maps in Minds.* New York: Harper & Row, 1977.

Gatty, H. *Nature Is Your Guide.* London: Collins, 1958.

Gladwin, T. *East Is a Big Bird.* Cambridge: Harvard University Press, 1970.

Hart, R. A. *Children's Experience of Place.* New York: Irvington, 1979.

Hart, R. A. "Children's Spatial Representation of the Landscape: Lessons and Questions from a Field Study." In L. S. Liben, A. H. Patterson, and N. Newcombe (Eds.), *Spatial Representation and Behavior Across the Life Span.* New York: Academic Press, 1981.

Hart, R. A., and Moore, G. T. "The Development of Spatial Cognition: A Review." In R. M. Downs and D. Stea (Eds.), *Image and Environment: Cognitive Mapping and Spatial Behavior.* Chicago: Aldine, 1973.

Herman, J. F. "Children's Cognitive Maps of Large-Scale Spaces: Effects of Exploration, Direction, and Repeated Experience." *Journal of Experimental Child Psychology,* 1980, *29,* 126–143.

Jerison, H. J. "Paleoneurology and the Evolution of Mind." *Scientific American,* 1976, *234,* 90–101.

Kirasic, K. C., Siegel, A. W., and Allen, G. L. "Developmental Changes in Recognition in Context Memory." *Child Development,* 1980, *51,* 302–305.

Kosslyn, S. M., Pick, H. L., and Fariello, G. R. "Cognitive Maps in Children and Men." *Child Development,* 1974, *45,* 707–716.

Lewin, K. *A Dynamic Theory of Personality.* New York: Academic Press, 1935.

Lewis, D. *We, the Navigators.* Honolulu: University Press of Hawaii, 1972.

Liben, L. S., Patterson, A. H., and Newcombe, N. (Eds.). *Spatial Representation and Behavior Across the Life Span.* New York: Academic Press, 1981.

Lord, F. E. "A Study of Spatial Orientation in Children." *Journal of Educational Research,* 1941, *34,* 481–505.

Maier, N. R. F. "Reasoning in Children." *Journal of Comparative Psychology,* 1936, *21,* 357–366.

Mead, G. H. *Mind, Self, and Society.* Chicago: University of Chicago Press, 1934.

Munn, N. D. *Walbiri Iconography: Graphic Representation and Cultural Symbolism in a Central Australian Society.* Ithaca, N.Y.: Cornell University Press, 1973.

Osgood, C. E. *Method and Theory in Experimental Psychology.* New York: Oxford University Press, 1953.

Pepper, S. C. *World Hypothesis.* Berkeley: University of California Press, 1970.

Piaget, J. *Biology and Knowledge.* Chicago: University of Chicago Press, 1971.

Piaget, J., and Inhelder, B. *The Child's Conception of Space.* New York: Norton, 1967.

Piaget, J., Inhelder, B., and Szeminska, A. *The Child's Conception of Geometry.* New York: Basic Books, 1960.

Reese, H. W., and Overton, W. F. "Models of Development and Theories of Development." In L. R. Goulet, and P. Baltes (Eds.), *Life Span Developmental Psychology: Research and Theory.* New York: Academic Press, 1970.

Rogoff, B., Sellers, M. J., Pirrotta, S., Fox, N., and White, S. H. "Age of Assignment of Roles and Responsibilities to Children: A Cross-Cultural Survey." *Human Development,* 1975, *18,* 353–369.

Siegel, A. W. "The Externalization of Cognitive Maps by Children and Adults: In Search of Ways to Ask Better Questions." In L. S. Liben, A. H. Patterson, and N. Newcombe (Eds.), *Spatial Representation and Behavior Across the Life Span.* New York: Academic Press, 1981.

Siegel, A. W., Allen, G. L., and Kirasic, K. C. "Children's Ability to Make Bidirectional Distance Comparisons: The Advantage of Thinking Ahead." *Developmental Psychology,* 1979, *15,* 656–657.

Siegel, A. W., and White, S. H. "The Development of Spatial Representations of Large-Scale Environments." In H. W. Reese (Ed.), *Advances in Child Development and Behavior.* Vol. 10. New York: Academic Press, 1975.

Siegel, A. W., and White, S. H. "The Child Study Movement: Early Growth and Development of the Symbolized Child." Unpublished manuscript, Department of Psychology and Social Relations, Harvard University, 1981.

Sigel, I. E., and Cocking, R. R. *Cognitive Development from Childhood to Adolescence: A Constructivist Perspective.* New York: Holt, Rinehart and Winston, 1977.

Trowbridge, C. C. "Fundamental Methods of Orientation and Imagery Maps." *Science,* 1913, *38,* 888–897.

von Uexkull, J. "A Stroll Through the Worlds of Animals and Men: A Picture Book of

Invisible Worlds." In C. H. Schiller (Ed. and Trans.), *Instinctive Behavior.* New York: International Universities Press, 1957.

Wapner, S. "Toward an Analysis of Transactions of Persons in a High Speed Society." Paper presented at a Symposium on "Man and a High Speed Society" sponsored by the International Association of Traffic and Safety Science, Tokyo, Japan, September 1980.

Wapner, S., Kaplan, B., and Ciottone, R. "Self-World Relationships in Critical Environmental Transitions: Childhood and Beyond." In L. S. Liben, A. H. Patterson, and N. Newcombe (Eds.), *Spatial Representation and Behavior Across the Life Span.* New York: Academic Press, 1981.

Wapner, S., Kaplan, B., and Cohen, C. B. "An Organismic-Developmental Perspective for Understanding Transactions of Men and Environments." *Environment and Behavior,* 1973, *5,* 255–289.

Werner, H. *Comparative Psychology of Mental Development.* New York: International Universities Press, 1957. (Originally published, 1948).

Werner, H., and Kaplan, B. *Symbol Formation.* New York: Wiley, 1963.

White, R. "Motivation Reconsidered: The Concept of Competence." *Psychological Review,* 1959, *66,* 297–333.

White, S. H. "Cognitive Competence and Performance in Everyday Environments." *Bulletin of the Orton Society,* 1980, *30,* 29–45.

White, S. H., and Siegel, A. W. "Cognitive Development in Time and Space." In B. Rogoff and J. Lave (Eds.), *Everyday Cognition: Its Development in Social Context.* Cambridge: Harvard University Press, 1982.

Whiting, B. B. "Culture and Social Behavior: A Model for the Development of Social Behavior." *Ethos,* 1980, *8,* 95–116.

Alexander W. Siegel is professor of psychology and director of the training program in developmental psychology at the University of Houston. His research interests include spatial cognition, developmental theory, and the history of developmental psychology.

Index

A

Accuracy, concept of, 90
Acredolo, L. P., 1, 3, 6, 11, 12, 13, 14, 15-16, 19-30, 45, 46, 49, 54, 63, 67, 68, 72, 77-78, 79, 83, 85, 86, 87, 88, 89, 92
Activity: analysis of, 41-50; implications of, 48-49; interaction-linked, 47-48; limits of role of, 44-45; and nature of environment, 46-48; prescribed, 43-44; research on role of, 42-48; summary of findings on, 45-46, 47. *See also* Locomotion
Adults: and activity research, 42-44, 47; and cognitive development, 70-71, 72, 73, 74, 75-76, 77, 78; and familiarity, 21-22, 24-25; and route knowledge, 33-37; in scale research, 8, 9, 10, 11; and spatial representation, 56-58, 59, 60-61
Ainsworth, M. D. S., 27, 28
Allen, G. L., 2, 17, 21, 28, 31-39, 50, 65, 66, 73, 74, 87, 88, 92, 93
Anderson, J. R., 79
Anooshian, L. J., 8, 14, 16, 26, 29
Appleyard, D., 10, 16, 20, 22, 26, 29
Array differentiation, 14
Array rotation, 13
Array shielding, 14
Attachment, and familiarity, 27-28

B

Baird, J. C., 59, 63
Baldwin, L. M., 11, 16, 26, 29, 35, 38, 43, 49
Barker, R. G., 85, 86, 89, 92
Barriers: and activity, 42-49; and spatial representation, 60-62
Bassett, E., 13, 16
Beck, R. J., 22, 24, 25, 26, 29
Bell, S. M., 27, 28
Benson, J. B., 23-24, 29
Berger, P. L., 90, 92
Bisanz, J., 32, 38

Blaut, J. M., 55, 64
Blind child, and Euclidian reference systems, 72
Borke, H., 7, 14, 16
Bossard, J. H. S., 88, 92
Bowlby, J., 27, 29
Bowles, N., 69, 79
Bremner, J. G., 25, 29
Breslow, L., 75, 79
Bridges, E., 70, 79
Brodzinsky, D., 7, 14, 16
Bronfenbrenner, U., 66-67, 79, 85, 92
Brown, A. L., 32, 38
Bruner, J. S., 90, 92
Bryant, K. H., 24, 25, 26, 29
Bryant, P. E., 25, 29, 75, 79
Burroughs, W. J., 22, 26, 30, 74, 80
Butler, P. A., 75, 76, 79
Byrd, D., 9. 16, 35, 44-45, 46, 48, 49

C

Carey, R., 7, 17
Chaiklin, S., 73, 80
Chaubaud, S., 70, 79
Children: social contexts of, 85-86; travel of, 86-89; at six months, 67; at seven months, 67; at nine months, 26-27, 67-78; at ten months, 23-24; at one and a half, 23; at two, 27-28; at two and a half, 72; at three, 11-12, 72, 74-75; at three and a half, 23; at four, 11-12, 24, 72, 74-75, 89; at five, 11-12, 21, 74-75; at six, 74-75, 89; at seven, 21, 33-37, 88; at eight, 24, 72, 89; at nine, 23, 43, 88; at ten, 21, 23, 33-37, 43; in infancy, 25; in preschool, 11, 23, 42-43, 53, 56-58, 72, 87; in kindergarten, 7-8, 9-10, 45, 56, 60, 72, 87; in first grade, 7-8, 10, 47-48, 60-61, 68; in second grade, 9, 10, 43-45, 72; in third grade, 7-8, 9-10, 12, 46; in fifth grade, 9, 10, 12, 45, 72; in sixth grade, 43-45, 46, 47-48, 68
Ciottone, R., 87, 94
Cocking, R. R., 86, 93

Cognitive development: analysis of, 65–81; class inclusion issues in, 70; social context of, 84–86

Cognitive mapping: and cartographic maps, 89–92; concept of, 6; conclusions on, 14; in large-scale space, 10–11; in model/small-scale space, 7–8; in navigable/small-scale space, 9–10; social ecology of, 83–94; and social learning, 88–89; and travel in social world, 86–89; and wayfinding, 90

Cohen, C. B., 90, 94

Cohen, R., 1–3, 6, 8, 9, 11, 12, 13, 14, 15, 16, 18, 24, 26, 29, 33, 35, 38, 41–50, 65, 68, 71, 76, 85, 88

Cohen, S., 47, 49

Cole, M., 85, 92

Collins, A. M., 37, 38

Commutativity, and configurational knowledge, 74

Configurational knowledge: development of, 74–76; route knowledge distinct from, 32

Corter, C. M., 25, 29

Coupe, P., 73, 80

Coyne, A. C., 8–9, 10, 13, 17

Curtis, L. E., 32, 38, 51n, 59, 63, 74, 79, 88, 92

D

Dayton, C. M., 7, 16

Dean, A. L., 70, 79

Development: conclusions on, 77–78; of configurational knowledge, 74–76; and familiarity, 21, 25; and perspective taking, 13; and route knowledge, 32–33, 34, 36–37; and spatial cognition, 52–53, 55, 65–81; stage and sequence in, 69–78

Dewey, J., 85, 92

Differentiation, and cognitive development, 72

Distance: and activity, 42–49; conservation of, 76–77; rank ordering of, 60–61; and route knowledge, 35–37

Douglas, M., 85, 92

Downs, R. M., 51n, 54, 55, 59, 62, 63, 74, 79, 84, 89, 90, 92

Dundon, W., 65n

E

Eliot, J., 7, 16

Euclidean concepts, 51–52, 71–74

Evans, D., 25, 28

Evans, G. W., 21, 24–25, 29, 75, 76, 79

Evocation, and route knowledge, 34–35

Exposure: active versus passive, 22–24, 44–45; amount of, 21–22, 44; and incidental or intentional learning, 24; and number of vantage points, 24–25; types of, 22–25, 44

F

Familiarity: and active versus passive exposure, 22–24; and affective factors, 26–28; analysis of, 19–30; concepts of, 19–20; as dependent variable, 20, 21–26; and development, 21, 25; and environment, nature of, 25–26; and exposure amount, 21–22; and exposure type, 22–25; and incidental versus intentional learning, 24; as independent variable, 19, 20–21; and number of vantage points, 24–25; and observer characteristics, 25; and security, 26–28, 67–68; what breeds it, 21–26; what it breeds, 20–21

Fariello, G. R., 10–11, 17, 26, 29, 35, 39, 42–43, 50, 59, 60, 61, 63, 76, 80, 83, 93

Fehr, L., 7, 16

Feldman, A. L., 11, 16, 23, 29, 45, 46, 49

Feldman, D. H., 71, 79

Fischer, K. W., 71, 79

Fishbein, H., 7, 13, 16, 17

Flavell, J. H., 7, 17, 34, 38, 53, 63, 70

Fox, N., 93

Furlong, N. E., 32, 38, 59, 63, 74, 79, 88, 92

G

Galligan, R. F., 25, 29

Gatty, H., 91, 92

Gauvain, M., 65n

Gibson, E. J., 32, 38

Gladwin, T., 90, 91, 92

Glanzer, M., 69, 79

Gleitman, H., 72, 78, 80

Golbeck, S. L., 56, 63, 72, 80

Golledge, R. G., 20, 29

Greenwald, J., 29

Grieve, R., 70, 80

H

Hardwick, D. A., 9, 10, 13, 14, 16, 59, 63

Harris, L. J., 48, 49
Harris, P., 13, 16
Hart, R. A., 1, 3, 23, 29, 31, 32, 38, 76, 78, 79, 83, 87, 91, 92–93
Hazen, N. L., 6, 11, 14, 16, 23, 29, 31, 32, 39, 74–75, 79
Herman, J. F., 6, 8–9, 10, 13, 14, 15, 16, 17, 21, 28, 29, 38, 45, 46, 49, 50, 72, 79, 87, 92, 93
Hood, L., 85, 92
Hoy, E., 7, 17
Hughes, M., 70, 80
Huttonlocher, J., 13, 14, 17, 75, 79

I

Inhelder, B., 7, 10, 13, 17, 39, 51–52, 53, 54, 56, 62, 63, 65, 71, 80, 88, 89, 91, 93
Istomina, Z. M., 68, 80
Ittelson, W. H., 1, 3, 5, 15, 17, 42, 50

J

Jackson, J., 7, 14, 16
Jerison, H. J., 90, 93

K

Kagan, S., 7, 17
Kahane, D., 14, 17
Kail, R. V., 20, 21, 25, 30, 32, 39, 41, 48, 50, 55, 64
Kaplan, B., 86, 87, 90, 94
Keesler, S., 29
Keiffer, K., 7, 16
Keller, R. A., 75, 80
Kirasic, K. C., 17, 20, 21, 25, 28, 30, 32, 38, 39, 41, 48, 50, 55, 64, 87, 92, 93
Knudson, K., 7, 17
Koeller, K., 16, 49
Kosslyn, S. M., 10–11, 17, 26, 29, 35, 39, 42–43, 50, 59, 60, 61, 63, 76, 80, 83, 93
Kozlowski, L. T., 24, 25, 26, 29

L

Laboratory of Comparative Human Cognition, 67, 80
Ladd, F. C., 10, 17
Landau, B., 72, 78, 80
Landmarks: and familiarity, 20–21; as reference points, 22; and route knowledge, 33–35

Large-scale spaces: activity in, 41–50; cognitive mapping in, 10–11; defined, 6; development of cognition of, 65–81; and familiarity, 19–30; model/small-scale space compared with, 76–77; navigable/small-scale space compared with, 12, 45; perspective taking in, 10; research on, 10–11; and route knowledge, 31–39; and spatial representation, 51–64; understanding of, 1–3
Laurendeau, M., 52, 63
Lee, T. R., 23, 29, 42, 50
Length, conservation of, 77
Lerner, R. M., 69, 80
Lewin, K., 85, 93
Lewis, D., 90, 91, 93
Lewis, S., 7, 16
Liben, L. S., 2, 7, 17, 27, 42, 46, 48, 50, 51–64, 65, 68, 69, 71, 72, 73, 76, 77, 80, 84, 91, 93
Lockman, J. J., 6, 11, 14, 16, 31, 32, 39
Locomotion: and cognitive mapping, 9–10; and perceptual feedback, 56; and perspective taking, 8, 14; and spatial representation, 54–58. *See also* Activity
Loftus, E. F., 37, 38
Lomenick, T., 16, 49
Lord, F. E., 83, 93
Luckmann, T., 90, 92
Luria, A. R., 37, 39
Lynch, K., 26, 29

M

McDermott, R., 85, 92
McGarrigle, J., 70, 80
McIntyre, C. W., 9, 10, 13, 14, 16, 59, 63
McKenna, W., 29
Magel, S. G., 77, 80
Maier, N. R. F., 83, 93
Maki, R. H., 73, 80
Mandler, G., 69, 80
Mandler, J. M., 32, 39
Maps: cartographic and cognitive, 89–92; of social world, 87–88
Markman, E., 70, 80
Marrerro, D. G., 75, 76, 79
Meacham, J., 68, 80
Mead, G. H., 90, 93
Merrill, A. A., 59, 63
Microgenesis, and ontogenesis, 71, 79
Milgram, S., 21–22, 26, 29
Miller, J., 7, 17

Minnigerode, F., 7, 17

Mnemonic strategies: and cognitive mapping, 7–8; and route knowledge, 37

Model/small-scale space: cognitive mapping in, 7–8; concept of, 6; and familiarity, 21; large-scale space compared with, 76–77; limitations of, 15; navigable/small-scale space compared with, 11–12; perspective taking in, 7; research on, 6–8

Moore, G. T., 1, 3, 31, 32, 38, 83, 91, 93

Moore, M. M., 56, 63, 72, 80

Munn, N. D., 89, 93

N

National Institutes of Health, Biomedical Research Support Grant from, 51n

Navigable/small-scale space: cognitive mapping in, 9–10; concept of, 6; large-scale space compared with, 12, 45; model/small-scale space compared with, 11–12; perspective taking in, 8–9; research on, 8–10

Nelson, T. O., 73, 80

New York City, familiarity with, 21–22

Newcombe, N., 2, 42, 50, 51n, 54, 60–61, 63, 65–81, 84, 93

Newman, J. L., 62, 63

Nigl, A., 7, 13, 17

O

Olsen, M. G., 11, 16, 19–20, 24, 28, 54, 63, 72, 79, 83, 92

Ontogenesis, and microgenesis, 71, 79

Osgood, C. E., 87, 93

Overton, W. F., 7, 14, 16, 62, 63, 90, 93

P

Parnicky, J. J., 29

Patterson, A. H., 42, 50, 84, 93

Pepper, S. C., 90, 93

Perspective taking: concept of, 6; conclusions on, 13–14; as developmental, 13; in large-scale space, 10; in model/small-scale space, 7; in navigable/small-scale space, 8–9

Peterson, H., 26, 29

Pezdek, K., 24–25, 29

Piaget, J., 7, 10, 13, 17, 32, 39, 51–52, 53, 54, 55, 56, 62, 63, 65, 70, 71, 76, 77, 80, 87, 88, 89, 90, 91, 93

Pick, H. L., 6, 19, 10–11, 13, 14, 16, 17, 19–20, 24, 26, 28, 29, 31, 32, 35, 39, 42–43, 50, 54, 59, 60, 61, 63, 72, 76, 79, 80, 83, 92, 93

Pinard, A., 52, 63

Pirrotta, S., 93

Pittsburgh, University of, 51n

Potts, G. R., 75, 80

Presson, C., 13, 14, 17

Primary nodes, 20

Pufall, P., 14, 17

R

Rayner, J., 29

Reese, H. W., 90, 93

Resnick, L. B., 32, 38

Richardson, G. D., 29

Rieser, J., 25, 30

Riley, C. A., 38, 39

Robinson, C. A., 32, 39

Rogoff, B., 65n, 67, 80, 89, 93

Rooley, C. J., 75, 80

Rosinski, R. R., 21, 28

Route knowledge: analysis of, 31–39; and cognitive mapping, 8; concept of, 32; configurational knowledge distinct from, 32; and development, 32–33, 34, 36–37; empirical studies of, 33–37; focus on, 32–33; and landmarks, 33–35; linearity of, 37–38; significance of, 37–38; and subdivisions, 35–37

S

Sadalla, E. K., 22, 26, 30, 74, 77, 80

Salatas, H., 7, 17

Salkind, N., 7, 14, 17

Samuels, H., 27–28, 30

Scale: comparison studies of, 11–12; concepts of, 5–6; conclusions on, 13–15; spatial cognition as function of, 5–18

Schadler, M., 7–8, 11, 14, 17, 56, 57, 64

Schatzow, M., 14, 17

Security, and familiarity, 26–28, 67–68

Seibert, J., 70, 80

Sellers, M. J., 93

Sex differences: in activity, 48; in perspective taking, 8

Shantz, C., 7, 14, 17

Shaw, R., 14, 17
Shemyakin, F. N., 10, 17, 32, 39
Sherman, R. C., 11, 16, 26, 29, 35, 38, 43, 49
Shlechter, T., 7, 14, 17
Siegel, A. W., 1, 2, 3, 6, 9, 11, 12, 13, 16, 17, 20, 21, 25, 28, 29, 30, 31, 32, 37, 38, 39, 41, 42, 45, 46, 48, 49, 50, 53–54, 55, 56, 57, 58, 59, 63–64, 72, 74, 79, 80, 83–94
Siegler, R. S., 53, 64
Sigel, I. E., 86, 93
Size: microspatial versus macrospatial, 5, 13; spatial cognition as function of, 5–18
Small-scale space. *See* Model/small-scale space; Navigable/small-scale space
Socialization, and cognitive development, 85–86
Society for Research in Child Development, 1
Space: practical and conceptual types of, 54; processing demands of, 15
Spatial cognition: and activity, 41–50; and cognitive mapping, 83–94; and conservation of distance and length, 76–77; and context issues, 66–68; development of, 52–53, 55, 65–81; and familiarity, 19–30; focus of research on, 62; as function of size and scale, 5–18; future research on, 15, 28, 49, 63, 78–79; interactions in, 2; issues in addressing, 51–54; measurement issues in, 68–69; methodological concerns in, 66–69; new methods for assessing, 53–54, 59–62; route knowledge of, 31–39; scale in, comparison studies of, 11–12; stage and sequence in, 69–78; topological to Euclidean concepts in, 51–52, 71–74
Spatial inference, development of, 75
Spatial information, context of, 68
Spatial products, 55
Spatial representation: assessment of, 51–64; and barrier effects, 60–62; concept of, 55; conclusions on, 62–63; derived measures of, 58–62; and locomotion, 54–58
Spatial storage, 55
Spatial thought, 55
Spelke, E., 72, 78, 80
Staplin, L. J., 22, 26, 30, 74, 80
Stasz, C., 25, 30

Stea, D., 55, 63, 64, 90, 92
Stevens, A., 73, 80
Subdivision, and distance relations, 35–37
Szeminska, A., 10, 17, 52, 63, 88, 89, 93

T

Tannenbaum, J., 59, 63
Thorndyke, P. W., 25, 30
Tolman, E. C., 65, 80
Topological concepts, 51–52, 71–74
Trabasso, R., 38, 39
Trabasso, T. T., 38, 39, 75, 81
Transitive inference: and configurational knowledge, 74–75; and route knowledge, 38
Trowbridge, C. C., 83, 91, 93
Tversky, B., 26, 30, 76, 81

U

Utilization, and route knowledge, 34–35
Uzgiris, I. C., 23–24, 29

V

von Uexkull, J., 90, 93–94

W

Walking. *See* Activity
Wapner, S., 87, 89, 90, 94
Waters, J., 29
Watkins, B., 7–8, 14, 17
Watson, J., 7, 14, 17
Wayfinding: and cognitive mapping, 90; and spatial cognition, 53, 54–55
Weatherford, D. L., 1, 5–18, 29, 35, 38, 42, 43–45, 46, 48, 49, 50, 65, 85, 91
Werner, H., 71, 81, 86, 90, 91, 94
White, R., 89, 94
White, S. H., 1, 3, 20, 21, 25, 30, 31, 32, 37, 39, 42, 50, 74, 80, 83, 84, 85, 86, 87, 90, 93, 94
Whiting, B. B., 88–89, 94
Wilkinson, A., 70, 81
Wilson, E. G., 38, 39
Wilson, K. L., 8, 14, 16, 26, 29
Wood, D., 22, 24, 25, 26, 29
Wright, H. F., 85, 86, 89, 92

Y

Youniss, J., 14, 17, 75

Z

Zucker, K. J., 25, 29